THE SMALL COLLEGE IMPERATIVE

THE SMALL COLLEGE IMPERATIVE

Models for Sustainable Futures

Mary B. Marcy

Foreword by Richard Ekman

STERLING, VIRGINIA

Published by Stylus Publishing, LLC.
22883 Quicksilver Drive
Sterling, Virginia 20166-2019

Library of Congress Cataloging-in-Publication Data
The CIP for this text has been applied for.

13-digit ISBN: 978-1-62036-970-8 (cloth)
13-digit ISBN: 978-1-62036-971-5 (paperback)
13-digit ISBN: 978-1-62036-972-2 (library networkable e-edition)
13-digit ISBN: 978-1-62036-973-9 (consumer e-edition)

Printed in the United States of America

All first editions printed on acid-free paper
that meets the American National Standards Institute
Z39-48 Standard.

Bulk Purchases

Quantity discounts are available for use in workshops and
for staff development.

Call 1-800-232-0223

First Edition, 2020

CONTENTS

FOREWORD

For more than three decades, colleges and universities have been active participants in a genuinely competitive market, an experience that has made them more like the other major sectors of the economy, and less the owners of a privileged status bestowed by governments and by their own clientele. This changed posture has had many good effects, including an increased motivation for innovation, a persuasive rationale for college faculty and staff to assume heavier workloads and for universities to trim costs, and a dawning recognition of a relentless need to explain college to skeptical publics. But the changed circumstance has also had harmful effects. Politicians, in particular, have found that public criticism of higher education attracts votes, while some business leaders have promoted the view that the main measure of a successful education is the quality of the jobs that new graduates enter.

The best results of this period of competition has been the explosion of innovation. Today imaginative programs abound and, while some may ultimately prove not to be sustainable, the creativity that has been unleashed in these recent efforts is impressive. Moreover, American higher education, already known for the diversity among the 4,000 institutions it includes (not to be confused with the diversity of students that any single college enrolls), has expanded these options immeasurably. Private higher education's 700 smaller colleges especially can now point to an astounding array of different educational philosophies and delivery systems.

To many people, the recent decades of innovation appear to be a period of confusion, even anarchy, in higher education. Mary Marcy is not one of them. Her *The Small College Imperative* provides a much needed framework to understand the rich array of options and institutional types that have evolved during the recent generative period. Marcy explains these options with clarity about their historical evolution so that a reader can understand how and why these changes took place. She distinguishes five of colleges: traditional, integrative, distinctive, expansion, and distr d. She provides not only the criteria by which to characterize each ty college but also excellent real-life examples.

Why does it matter how we view the patterns into wh vative colleges can be classified? For those who lead colleges, this offer a helpful lens through which to see one's own college and its best path to future success. Any college president knows that one key to success is to offer a program that is distinctive and is widely perceived as distinctive. The challenge for that college president is to know what is truly distinctive. The guidance in planning that Marcy's screen of institutional types provides is highly valuable.

For prospective students and their parents, as well as for donors, legislators, and journalists, the categories that Marcy discerns and discusses offer a way to make sense of what otherwise may appear to be chaos. Choosing a college that is well matched to the interests, strengths, and gaps of a student's prior preparation is always a challenge for the student and often his or her parents. Marcy's typology will be helpful because it adds another filter to a choice among 4,000 institutions.

In any period of innovation, it's difficult to know which novel programs are most likely to prove durable. The Council of Independent Colleges has collected and grouped into categories hundreds of recent campus innovations in its 2018 report, *Innovation and the Independent College*. To say that this climate of innovation is stimulating to the faculty members and students who inhabit these institutions may be to state the obvious, but Marcy helps us to understand, less obviously, that all types of institutions can be simultaneously innovative and committed to certain principles of institutional mission and pedagogical practice that are common features of specific types of institutions.

The American small college has long held a reputation for nimble and entrepreneurial behavior. Marcy shows us what it can add up to. These small colleges are often the incubators of educational innovations that are eventually adopted by all colleges and universities. Marcy shows us the varieties of program that deliberate and creative choices of educational philosophies have produced, are available to students now, and will no doubt continue to evolve for many years to come.

Richard Ekman, President,
Council of Independent Colleges,
Washington, DC

o
e
types
ibute
e of

ch inn
typolog

ACKNOWLEDGMENTS

I t is not possible to write anything of substance as a sitting university president unless the board of trustees shares a belief in the value of the work and a commitment to advancing knowledge. I have been very fortunate to have a board of trustees that is not only supportive but also deeply committed to the work of independent colleges and universities. It was the board's request to place our work at Dominican University in a larger national context that planted the seeds for this project, it was the board's ongoing curiosity about the larger higher education landscape that invited deeper reflection, and it was the board's steady support—including support for a presidential sabbatical—that created the space and time for reflection necessary to create this book. It's leadership, generosity, and deep commitment to student success has helped realize both this book and the creation of the Dominican Experience.

In order to complete this work, I was fortunate to have a brief but productive presidential sabbatical at the Harvard Graduate School of Education (HGSE), where I served as a visiting scholar. My time at Harvard was enriched by the opportunity to work closely with Judith Block McLaughlin, the longtime leader of HGSE's higher education programs and a mentor to innumerable college and university presidents. Her wisdom and insight are exceeded only by her personal generosity. I am humbled and grateful to have such a colleague and friend.

Because of McLaughlin's thoughtfulness, at Harvard I also had the opportunity to work with eight exceptional graduate students who conducted much of the field work and initial writing for the campus profiles included in this book. As a group, their interest and engagement did much to strengthen the depth and scope of this work.

I have a senior leadership team at Dominican that is both highly skilled and highly collaborative. Its ideas have directly and indirectly influenced the development of my thinking and provided invaluable insight into the steps required to successfully move from vision to implementation. They also accepted significant new responsibilities while I pursued my visiting scholar work at Harvard; most notably Nicola Pitchford stepped ably into the role of acting president during my brief sabbatical. The President's Cabinet as a whole are deeply capable individual leaders, immeasurably strong colleagues, and an exceptional team. Both the sabbatical and the realization of this work were possible because of my confidence in them.

Any ability I might have to consider the context for small colleges and universities has been developed and nurtured through the good work of Richard Ekman and the Council of Independent Colleges (CIC). This organization not only serves as a leader and convening authority for the sector, but also conducts important ongoing research about independent colleges. Many of the ideas developed in this book began while I served as a member of the steering committee for CIC's Project on the Future of Independent Higher Education. Further information about the work of that group, further research on the innovations currently taking place at independent colleges, and comprehensive information about the sector can be found at www. cic.edu.

Through this project, I had the double good fortune of working with two extraordinary individuals at opposite stages of their careers in higher education. Alan Guskin is a man of wisdom, integrity, courage, good humor, and seemingly endless patience. For the last 20 years I have benefitted from his mentorship and colleagueship. Jennifer Krengel recently completed her master's degree and began working as a higher education professional only in the last few years. Her curiosity, research skills, insight, attention to detail, and gracious approach to issues large and small brought both clarity and quality to this effort. Without the help of Al and Jenn my analysis would be weaker; my thinking would be less complex; my references would be more incomplete; my schedule would be even more unmanageable; and this book, quite simply, would not exist.

THE SHIFTING LANDSCAPE

As a lapsed political scientist, I have a keen appreciation for the challenges of futurists. After all, a few decades ago we believed the American model of democracy was in the ascendant and poised to spread across the globe. A few years ago we thought increasingly sophisticated quantitative systems would make election outcomes, and their explanations, more predictable. Until recently, the European Union was seen as a lasting, stable solution to that continent's history of conflict. And these are just the prediction challenges of one discipline.

Today, there is no shortage of predictions, usually dire, about the future of small independent colleges and universities. And there is no shortage of rhetoric challenging the assumptions behind these forecasts. Are small colleges doomed to irrelevance in the face of changing demographics, a broken business model, and the rise of technology? Are the liberal arts an essential and enduring feature of higher education or an outdated luxury for the privileged elite?

This book does not attempt to add to the list of prognostications, nor does it offer a simple solution to the issues facing most independent colleges. Rather, in the midst of the angst and dire predictions about the future of small colleges, it attempts to move through the anxiety and outline ways in which small colleges can adapt, and in some cases *are* adapting, to a changing environment. The shifts in the landscape are not entirely new, but they have been accelerating in recent years, and understanding the major issues is essential to identifying how small colleges can best respond.

Perhaps, as I once suggested in previous writing, small colleges and universities are more akin to Broadway, that "fabulous invalid" whose demise has been regularly predicted, and yet somehow never realized. Broadway now thrives on a mixture of innovation (*Hamilton*), reinvention (jukebox musicals), and classic productions (*South Pacific*, anyone?). As we will see throughout this book, independent colleges and universities are also adopting multiple creative approaches as they seek a path to sustainability.

Small colleges and universities have already been actively responding to the changing environment, with various degrees of success. There is much to be learned from their emerging efforts. This book presents a taxonomy for organizing the approaches small independent colleges and universities are using to respond in order to understand the opportunities and issues inherent in each path.

After outlining the different approaches small colleges are employing to adapt to the shifting landscape, I offer a template for making key decisions about the future of an institution with questions that help contextualize the challenges and opportunities. While the environmental changes are felt across the country, the success of different responses is influenced by location, history, and type of campus. Context matters, and this template provides a means of evaluating the positions of specific campuses.

Finally, I consider the ways in which small colleges and universities are expanding their vision of consortia and partnerships in order to enhance both fiscal and educational sustainability. Regardless of an institution's position in the taxonomic framework, many campuses are adding to their internal innovations a fresh view of how to effectively link with other campuses or with other external partners.

Fundamental Changes in the Independent College Environment

While there are sometimes conflicting predictions about the fate of independent colleges and universities, there is little debate that the environment for these institutions is changing in ways that can challenge their missions, their institutional stability, and even their viability. These changes are affecting small colleges in much the way climate change is affecting our larger environment: slow (but accelerating), inexorable, and necessitating a fundamental shift in the way we operate. Any successful path forward must address these changing external realities.

A closer look at the shifts that are confronting the business and educational approach of independent colleges helps frame their dilemma. The pressures include four key factors: changing student demographics, a business model that no longer yields reliable growth, significant shifts in market demand for traditional liberal arts programs, and the expanding use of technology.

The first major recent change for small colleges and universities is a significant shift in demographics—in the profile, geographic location, a   ber—of young people who are of traditional college age. These demographic shifts are at the heart of the challenges facing small colleges, and declining birth rates indicate the problems will only accelerate in the next two decades. From the 1950s through the beginning of this century, college enrollment was fueled both by population growth and by an increase in the percentage of the population seeking college education. That growth has now leveled off or decreased, depending on region of the country (Western Interstate Commission for Higher Education, 2017).

Along with the flatlining of the traditional college-bound population is a changing student profile. Where there is some growth in the high school population, it is primarily in groups that have been historically underrepresented in higher education. The percentage and number of White students graduating from high school is decreasing, and that decrease is projected to continue. Meanwhile, Hispanic, Black, and Asian Pacific Island high school graduates are increasing gradually in raw numbers and significantly as a percentage of their graduating cohorts. This is a change in more than complexion. Compared to White children, Hispanic and Black children are twice as likely to be from low-income families and half as likely to have a college-educated parent (Western Interstate Commission for Higher Education, 2017).

This shift in student profile adds urgency to the quest for independent colleges and universities to adapt and remain viable. If higher education has been heralded as *the great equalizer*, then the increasing proportion of students who are low income, ethnically and racially diverse, or first-generation college challenges our institutions to live up to the promise of higher education as a means of personal opportunity and social change. The pressure for small colleges is particularly pertinent, for on the one hand, the environment of independent colleges makes them particularly well positioned to respond to an increasingly diverse student body; small classes and integrated support systems can be especially effective in promoting student success (Kuh, O'Donnell, & Reed, 2013). They are essential elements in providing the needed support for first-generation and underrepresented students. On the other hand, many small colleges were created for, and still primarily serve, middle- and upper-middle-class White students.

As we will see later in this book, some independent colleges and universities are effectively embracing the changing student population, with encouraging results. Chapters 5 and 6 include profiles of Trinity Washington University, Dominican University of California, and California Lutheran University. Each provides examples of differing, but effective, approaches to serving highly diverse student populations.

Adding to the challenge of the changing student profile and stagnation in growth of the traditional student population is a geographic challenge. Stated bluntly, independent colleges and universities are not located in areas where the population is growing. The brick-and-mortar locations of these campuses are largely in the Midwest and Northeast, the areas with the biggest decline in the college-going population. Figure 1.1, a simple map that integrates change in the college-age population and the location of members of the Council of Independent Colleges, highlights the misalignment.

The second major pressure that is facing most small colleges and universities is the failure of—or at least extreme stress on—the business model. Fundamentally, this means that the high-tuition, high-financial-aid approach to student enrollment is not yielding the same results that it did a decade or more ago. As both the sticker price and the tuition discount rate have steadily risen, the bottom line of net tuition revenue has barely shifted for nearly two decades. For tuition-driven institutions—a category that encompasses most small independent colleges—this stagnation has placed tremendous pressure on the business model, as illustrated in Figure 1.2.

The high-tuition, high-financial-aid model has always been dependent on a robust supply of middle- and upper-middle-income families that are able and willing to pay close to the full cost of their education. As the national wealth gap grows, and as more of those students aspiring to college are from lower-income families, there are fewer families in the pipeline with the capacity to pay full freight. In addition, many colleges find that, even if they are *able*, there are simply not enough families *willing* to pay the costs

Figure 1.1. Independent colleges and projected change in high school graduates, 2017 to 2023.

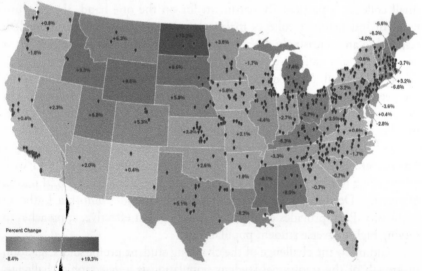

Note: Image produced by Margaret Wylie. Data from Council of Independent Colleges (2019) and Western Interstate Commission for Higher Education (2017).

Figure 1.2. Average published and net prices in 2018 dollars, full-time undergraduate students at private nonprofit four-year institutions, 1998–1999 to 2018–2019.

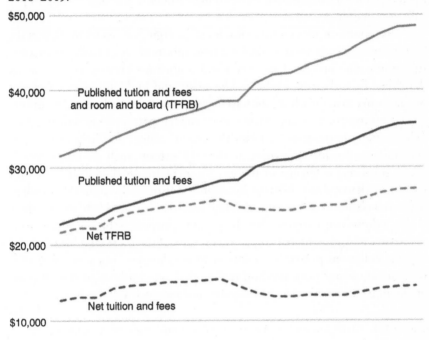

Note: Reproduced with permission from the College Board (2018).

of private higher education. Both of these factors have escalated as institutions ratchet up the high-tuition, high-aid model in hopes of gaining some additional revenue. And the problem has also escalated as campuses provide merit aid to bid for students regardless of their ability to pay. Savvy, reasonably financed, and well-coached families do not expect to pay the full cost of private college. Meanwhile, a growing number of students and families are simply unable to do so.

Some independent colleges have responded to this reality by implementing a tuition reset process; essentially, the institution decreases the sticker price and simultaneously reduces financial aid, in the hopes of increasing both enrollment and net tuition revenue. This approach is inconsistently successful and demands considerable assessment prior to implementation

(Lapovsky, 2019). Ultimately, both the high-tuition, high-aid approach and the reduced sticker price achieved through tuition resets face the same fundamental challenge: There need to be enough students able and willing to pay full, or near-full, price.

This book contains useful examples of emerging strategies to address the cost of college. In chapter 7 there is a description of Utica College's successful tuition reset process. Chapters 5 and 6 illustrate creative new strategies developed by California Lutheran University and by Dominican University of California to align scholarships to regional needs. And chapter 10 outlines several innovative new approaches to consortia, partnerships, and program delivery that are designed to lower the cost of college and help institutions and students develop alternatives to the high-tuition, high-aid framework.

A third major change in the environment for small colleges is a shift in market demand for different disciplines. Historically, attaining a college degree was considered both an individual asset and a social benefit, but there is now a dominant narrative that the primary purpose of higher education is to secure well-compensated employment. One of the most tangible results of viewing college as primarily a pathway to employment is a significant shift in demand toward programs and majors that are clearly aligned with postgraduation careers, as seen in Figure 1.3 and Figure 1.4.

Figure 1.3. Changing student demand for traditional academic programs.

NRCCUA major group trend
Interest levels are expected to change and stabilize as each class completes high school.

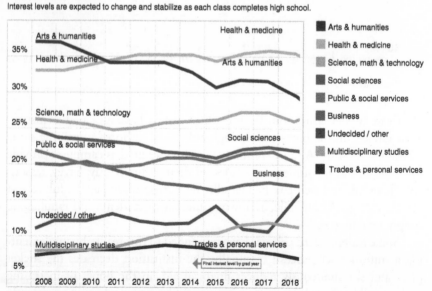

Note: Image courtesy of National Research Center for College & University Admissions, featuring data from WICHE and Encoura Data Lab by ACT (2016).

Figure 1.4. Change in degrees, 2011–2017.

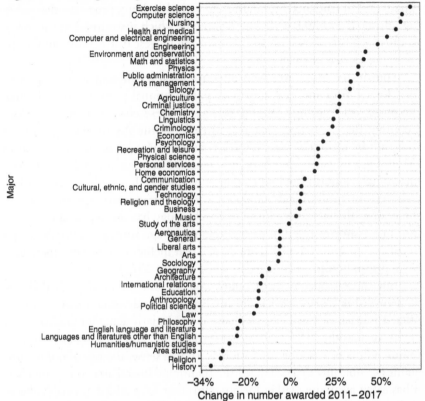

Sources: NCES IPEDS data; taxonomy adapted from American Academy of Arts and Sciences.

Note: Data from Schmidt (2018).

These data show a move away from the programs typically offered in the liberal arts curriculum and toward more instrumental degrees. The one ray of optimism for small liberal arts colleges in these data is the growth in "undecided," as students may still be going to college to find their path, rather than simply to fulfill the requirements for employment. Small colleges must either convince prospective students and parents that a liberal arts degree can lead to a good job, or must more consciously show the path to employment post-degree; in addition, many are adding programs that are in high demand and more obviously tied to specific careers.

The emerging models for small colleges and universities outlined in this book illustrate many ways in which these institutions are responding to the changes in demand for different programs and to the expectation that college will lead directly to employment. These responses range from building more systems that link the academic experience to career, to guided pathways to aid in students' exploration, to actively adding programs that are in high demand by employers. The manner in which institutions are adapting to career expectations represents one of the biggest distinctions among the emerging models of small colleges.

Fourth, the rapid evolution of educational technology and the growth of online courses and programs have put additional pressure on traditional campus-based learning. The full impact of these changes is not yet clear. Certainly the prediction that place-based institutions would be rendered irrelevant by technology has not come to pass. Massive open online courses (MOOCs), in particular, have not replaced campus-based learning. But increasingly sophisticated educational technology has built a new market, especially in professional retraining with nontraditional-age students. In some ways, the fact that educational technology has not replaced in-person learning reinforces the notion that traditional-age students still seek to "go to college" in some familiar manner, one that includes a range of experiences beyond simply courses and credentialing (Horn, 2019).

But the establishment of online courses and online degrees that can be delivered at lower cost has already begun to undermine many programs offered at small colleges. The challenge is particularly acute for graduate programs, such as the MBA and teacher certification, and for programs targeted toward adults or working professionals. In this sense, the rise of online programs has not directly challenged the traditional liberal arts core as much as it has eaten away the market for programs that were added at small colleges to diversify offerings and strengthen the bottom line.

Later in this book we will see that the role and use of educational technology is a central question for institutions to answer as they determine a viable path forward. Chapters 7 and 8 illustrate the ways in which some institutions have actively used technology to expand, and the accompanying profiles of Utica College and Southern New Hampshire University show this strategy in action. The development of educational technology continues at a rapid pace, led by companies interested in scale and hungry for new markets. There is little doubt this change will continue to affect the business and educational model of small colleges and universities, even if the specific ways in which it will influence these campuses is more difficult to predict.

How campuses have responded to this challenging environment in the short term, and how they can build a sustainable financial and educational model for the long term, is the focus of this book. The story is a complex one, but it contains the seeds of innovation and possibility that can offer a hopeful future for many institutions.

2

FROM SURVIVAL TO SUSTAINABILITY

A s we have seen, the landscape for small private colleges and universities has changed dramatically in recent years. These shifts have put considerable pressure on the usual work of leading a campus, as leaders try to navigate a rapidly changing environment, maintain fidelity to mission and shared governance, and envision a fiscally sustainable and academically robust future for the campus.

To appreciate the ways in which the changing environment is putting pressure on campuses, it is helpful to understand the operating model most institutions have used in their annual budgeting and planning. Most of our institutional systems were developed to assume modest, steady growth in the base operating budget; for small colleges without large endowments, that growth is expected to be driven largely by net tuition revenue. Budgets are built each year based on assumptions of minimal changes and slow but predictable growth. For years, colleges were the certificates of deposit of the higher education world, using reliable, if undramatic, growth to maintain health. The role of campus leadership in this environment was to wisely steward that growth, while using fundraising to test or expand new initiatives on the margin.

Success in this financial and educational structure has never been simple, but the model itself relies on relative predictability. Modest but steady increases in tuition lead to increased net tuition revenue, which in turn allows for investment in compensation, professional development, student support, tenure-line faculty, and the maintenance of a low student-to-faculty ratio. Effective management of the endowment yields reliable growth and adds to the physical and operational capacity of the institution. Fundraising campaigns support major capital expenditures, secure endowed funds for scholarships and chairs, and underwrite significant innovations. The ongoing work of the finance office is to ensure balanced budgets and clean audits and to preserve the character of the institution. New systems, programs, or initiatives are welcomed as additions to the existing model, but explicitly do not bring any changes to that model.

The work of leading a campus that is able to maintain steady, modest revenue growth and reliable enrollment numbers is the work of stewardship: ensuring a strong educational environment by investing in tenure-line faculty and qualified staff, meeting budget and enrollment targets, preserving or building the endowment, managing ongoing maintenance, securing accreditation at the institutional and appropriate programmatic levels, and fundraising for new programs and buildings.

Figure 2.1 captures the assumptions and actions that are typical at most campuses in an environment focused on stewardship.

Leading in a climate focused on stewardship is complex. It pits competing priorities and aspirations against each other in a system with only modest growth. In an industry where research and expansion aspirations are normal and rewarded, the competition can be fierce. At a higher education conference in the 1990s, I heard, president of Harvard at the time, Neil Rudenstine remark that his university simply did not have enough resources. When the audience began to chuckle, he acknowledged it is "all a matter of perspective and ambition." There are always more demands for new projects than there are new resources, even at the most financially robust institutions; some of the more elite institutions in the country have faced financial challenges and occasionally even run major deficits.

But while success has not been simple to accomplish in the stewardship mode, it is relatively easy to measure. Historically, success in this model has meant expanding resources and reputation beyond the existing assumptions. Thus, success has been measured through dramatic fundraising coups; larger-than-anticipated enrollment boosts or increased selectivity; perceived

Figure 2.1. Stewardship strategies.

Stewardship
• Build endowment
• Balance budgets
• Manage deferred maintenance
• Maintain low student-faculty ratio
• Commit to tenure lines
• Fundraise for new projects
• New projects are add-ons

Note: Marcy (2017b).

improvement in status, sometimes including movement up the ranks of *U.S. News & World Report;* or the addition of creative new programs and initiatives.

The problem is that, even with the most adept leadership, this kind of success is simply no longer enough. Over the last two decades, and especially since the great recession, the traditional approach has not served small colleges and universities well. In 2009, at the nadir of the recession, I participated in a gathering of college and university presidents. The mood was captured by the well-respected president of a highly selective small college, who reflected, "I always thought I knew how my presidential obituary would read. Now I'm not so sure."

And while the most financially secure and elite campuses have recovered from the recession, the majority of small colleges and universities have not. Simply stated, the stewardship model no longer works at most institutions, as evidenced by the flatlining of net tuition revenue illustrated in the previous chapter. Even as campuses have become increasingly adept at fundraising, and presidents have developed ever more aggressive schedules and strategies for growth, in too many cases their work has not fundamentally advanced their institutions. Activities that in the past would have dramatically improved the status of an institution are now necessary just for ensuring ongoing operations. Changing demographics, shifting market expectations, and intensifying financial pressures are overwhelming the ability of any but the wealthiest institutions to subsist effectively in the stewardship mode. Particularly in the last few years, most small institutions have not been able to operate entirely, or even primarily, from a position of stewardship. They have operated from a position of maintenance at best and, in some cases, simply for survival.

Initial Responses to the Changing Environment: Austerity

As campus leaders adapt to this changing environment—and to the subsequent pressure on fiscal and educational viability—they have initially implemented measures focused on budget reduction and control. In response to an environment that no longer offers sufficient resources to support the usual mode of operations, campuses have become fiscally austere and creative at the margins, as they seek to find efficiencies on the one hand and new sources of revenue on the other.

Just as institutions in stewardship mode take similar approaches to fiscal and educational management, campus responses to austerity have been fairly consistent across institutions. To adapt to an environment of constrained resources, campuses reduce nonpersonnel costs in an attempt to protect jobs while managing the budget. These restrictions are often accompanied by hiring freezes in nonfaculty positions. On the academic side, hiring adjunct faculty rather than tenure-line faculty to cover curricular requirements becomes the rule rather than the exception. Services such as maintenance, food operations, the bookstore, security, the library, and student housing are contracted out or reviewed with an eye toward collaboration and cost-sharing with other institutions. If the campus has a significant debt load, leaders will attempt to refinance that debt at a more competitive rate. The campus may run operating deficits or take unusually large endowment draws to weather the storm.

The typical response to a changing fiscal environment also includes standard revenue generation efforts. Enrollment targets and tuition setting receive intense attention, with a focus on net tuition dollars. Meanwhile, bidding intensifies for the small pool of coveted students who are both academically qualified and financially able to cover more than the discounted cost of their degree. Nondegree programs and campus rentals become increasingly important to the bottom line. And fundraising efforts become more aggressive as annual fund goals are used to balance budgets.

Figure 2.2 outlines the most common austerity strategies used by campuses that are facing budget challenges.

These measures are useful, even strategic, in the short term. They can offer modest room in a tight budget. In slightly difficult years, they may provide enough capacity for cost-of-living salary adjustments or investment in innovation. In more difficult years, they may mean the difference between a challenging budget and a disastrous one. Continuing to tighten resources, reset budgets, and search for efficiencies can be a productive strategy if there is clarity that it is short-term and the long-term plan for fiscal stability is clear and achievable.

Figure 2.2. Austerity strategies.

Austerity
• Reduce nonpersonnel expenses
• Hire more part-time faculty
• Increase tuition
• Increase enrollment
• Contract out select services
• Intensify fundraising
• Refinance debt
• Defer maintenance
• Draw largely on endowment

Marcy (2017b).

But too often these are not short-term actions. Instead, they may be practiced year after year, either because there is a lack of long-term vision or there is an assumption—implicit or explicit—that the campus will return to the days of stewardship. And as we have seen, the demographic, financial, and market trends make such a return unlikely at best for the majority of campuses.

Meanwhile, austerity practiced over a long period of time can have debilitating long-term consequences. When used as a year-after-year operating model, these austerity strategies can do real damage. The consequences are manifest, and they are multiplying. For example, in the traditional approach to education at small colleges, the vast majority of courses were taught by tenure-line faculty, and adjuncts were hired for their targeted expertise or to manage unanticipated enrollment ripples. But in recent years, adjuncts have been hired not based on this targeted approach, but as a means to cover required courses and balance the budget. The result has been a dramatic increase in the adjunct population at small colleges, with corresponding negative effects. The recent wave of unionization of nontenure-line faculty has highlighted the large number of poorly supported adjuncts on many campuses; the deleterious impact on both faculty lives and student learning; and the challenges of using this approach as a long-term strategy to manage budgets, curriculum, and personnel.

On the revenue producing side, fundraising for the yearly operating budget should be based on year-over-year performance, with reasonable expectations for modest growth. Instead, many campuses have invested heavily in the fundraising effort, pushed their annual fund goals to unrealistic levels, and managed disappointing results through higher endowment draws or budgeting unrealized gifts. Over time the endowment is no longer above water, and budgeting for estate gifts is unpredictable: More than one campus president has remarked that the best assurance of a long life for a philanthropist seems to be a testamentary gift agreement with their institution.

There are similar problems with all of these budget management tactics. Short-term responses to budget challenges do not lead to long-term sustainability. At some point, there is no more fat to be cut from administration, the pool of adjunct faculty cannot continue to grow, the stock of full-pay students withers, the debt has been refinanced, and the certificate market has been saturated. Meanwhile, over time austerity can eat away at campus morale, threaten shared governance, and undermine educational quality. The consequences for educational quality and institutional health are serious, and can even threaten the long-term survival of institutions.

To be clear, short-term tactics are effective and can be necessary if the long-term future of the institution is being developed *at the same time*. But how does a campus move through austerity while developing a vision for the future, one that provides a realistic business model and ensures quality education? In an environment of fiscal austerity, shifting student demographics, and unsustainable college pricing, what is the long-term solution?

One response is to assume the campus can return to the days of stewardship, where a revived external environment, more effective student recruitment, and deft fundraising will lead to a return to stable budgets and accustomed educational norms. This approach is what colleagues and I labeled, in earlier writing, "muddling through," the assumption that after hunkering down for a few difficult years, things will return to normal and the campus can resume conventional operations; in other words, stewardship (Guskin & Marcy, 2003). This may still be possible for some campuses, but the reality is that it is a likely scenario for very, very few. As Steven Mintz (2014) argues,

> These strategies work less well for less prestigious institutions. For these universities, a model built around the concept of more—more programs, more buildings, more grants and contracts, and more residential students—has done little to improve affordability, access, and student success. Nor has this approach enhanced institutional sustainability. Clearly, new models are necessary.

Strategic reductions may allow an institution to muddle through for a while. But—barring a dramatic change in fiscal, demographic, and market realities—they will not return the campus to the days of stewardship or to fiscal stability and academic excellence.

Toward Models of Sustainability

The imperative for most campuses is to adapt to the new environment through some type of change in the institutional business and education model. For most, this will require substantial change. The process of moving an institution from survival to long-term sustainability and the differences in approach at each stage are captured in Figure 2.3.

Sustainability in this model has several meanings. Certainly the long-term vision must be financially sustainable; the lack of financial equilibrium is, in large part, what necessitates change. But sustainability of mission and of educational quality requires a slightly different frame. If possible, the purpose of the institution and its distinctive educational contributions should be preserved in the midst of change; they provided the reasons for the creation

Figure 2.3. Moving from survival to sustainability.

	Stewardship	Austerity	Strategic Vision
Actions	• Build endowment • Balance budgets • Manage deferred maintenance • Maintain low student-to-faculty ratio • Commit to tenure lines • Fundraise for new projects • Add on new projects as needd	• Reduce nonpersonnel expenses • Hire more part-time faculty • Increase tuition • Increase enrollment • Contract out select services • Intensify fundraising • Refinance debt • Defer maintenance • Draw largely on endowments	**Assess:** • Affirm essential elements of mission • Identify institutional strengths • Evaluate student demographics and landscape **Select:** • Choose the most promising model of change • Create strategic vision **Transform:** • Develop multiyear sustainable budget models • Align programs and systems • Align fundraising and marketing

of the campus and offer the justification for its continued existence. Purity of historic offerings may not be possible, but most campuses can point to essential values and academic strengths that are central to the institution's purpose.

When these essential campus characteristics are identified, the campus can evolve other aspects of its programs and systems to adapt to the demands of a new environment. For small colleges and universities, this process must focus on student learning. A realistic assessment of the profile of current and prospective students is important for understanding how to develop an educational and financial model that will serve them well. Campuses must also identify an academic program mix that resolves changing market demand with institutional strengths and history. Support systems and programs should be aligned to respond to these strengths and to the emerging student demographic. And multiyear budgets, fundraising, and marketing should be aligned with the long-term vision of the campus.

Undertaking substantial change while preserving institutional identity is challenging but attainable. The key is to understand the aspects of mission and identity that are essential elements of the institution, while adapting, when necessary, the manner in which those core values are delivered.

Along with research and analysis, shared governance and outreach to major constituencies are central to creating a viable vision for the future. This outreach helps rather than hinders the process of change, because a sustainable vision must include the investment of key stakeholders across the institution. This means that developing and implementing this vision takes time, but, with markers of progress and momentum, the change can be realized. Of course, some campuses do not believe they have time for the shared governance process. Campuses that require radical transformation in order to stabilize or survive often undergo rapid change, sometimes including changing mission or seeking mergers. Later chapters will include examples of campuses that have actively embraced shared governance and implemented shifts over several years and others that have moved more quickly and radically to respond to looming threats.

Paradoxically, to move to a more sustainable model, campus leaders need to embrace strong stewardship and also need to utilize some of the short-term tactics of fiscal austerity, all while building a compelling long-term vision of academic quality and fiscal equilibrium. This is work that must happen simultaneously, with a clear eye toward the external environment and the health of the institution. It is imperative that campus leaders recognize the difference between short-term tactics and long-term solutions, *even as they practice both*. They must guide an evolution from stewardship of campus mission, to short-term preservation, and ultimately to sustainability.

Fundamental change requires more than year-to-year adjustment; it requires a vision for the long-term health of the institution. A number of campuses have begun to develop new approaches for institutional quality and sustainability. The viability of these approaches depends on the location and existing characteristics of an institution, as well as effective leadership. As the pressures on independent colleges and universities have become more acute, changes to the business and academic program are being tested.

There is much to learn from the emerging innovations being employed at independent colleges and universities. The next chapter presents a taxonomy of institutional innovations and outlines the most common approaches by category. In subsequent chapters I will evaluate the effectiveness of various models for both educational quality and fiscal stability, and consider the leadership needed to realize successful institutional change.

3

FIVE EMERGING MODELS OF SMALL COLLEGES AND UNIVERSITIES

Many small colleges and universities have been managing in the midst of uncertainty, and often austerity, in recent years. Some are facing immediate financial challenges. Others are running unsustainable structural deficits that presage serious consequences for the future. And as we have seen, to build a viable long-term future, most must also realize fundamental change; change that adapts to the evolving realities of cost, demographics, markets, and emerging technology; change that recognizes these issues are not short term or temporary, but long term and structural.

There are several consistent tools, beyond austerity, that campuses typically use to respond to the changing environment. They include adding new locations, adding new programs, changing delivery modalities, changing campus educational approaches, and adjusting the business model.

More specifically, to reach more students, an institution may add new locations or sites with focused programs that serve the particular needs of an area; for example, a campus may open a new off-campus site delivering only evening business courses or offering teacher education to an underserved area.

Many campuses create new academic programs that are designed to respond to emerging market demand. These new programs are often aligned with not only shifting student interests, but also business cycles and the employment market in the local area.

Campuses that change delivery modalities use increasingly sophisticated technology to add online programs or to create hybrid programs.

These programs frequently build from existing traditional campus programs with high demand or are developed in areas of particular strength for the institution.

And some campuses are shifting their on-campus educational focus to be more student oriented rather than program oriented. These institutions are employing emerging research about the most effective practices in teaching and learning, with a particular emphasis on responding to changing student demographics and changing expectations of college.

Campuses that address the business model itself are usually trying to shift the pricing model to provide some relief from the high-tuition, high-financial-aid approach. The most common change is a tuition reset, a process that entails lowering the sticker price, and also lowering financial aid, in the hopes of driving up total enrollment and net tuition revenue. Some campuses are also experimenting with more cross-campus collaboration to lower cost and exploring innovative new partnerships and consortia.

In the following chapters we will see all of these approaches in action. Many of these tactics can be helpful as campuses adapt to an increasingly difficult environment. But they are not, by themselves, a sustainable strategy for responding to the headwinds facing small colleges and universities. A long-term strategy for sustainability requires a more thoughtful, comprehensive approach, one that employs some of these tactics but moves beyond them. To actually create a sustainable future, change must also be integrated, comprehensive, and multifaceted.

While many campuses are doing their best simply to muddle through, a number have begun to adopt more long-term and comprehensive strategies as they respond to the changing environment. Their approaches range from minor tweaks to fundamental transformation. Sometimes through planning and sometimes through the accreted consequences of muddling through over time, these responses have often resulted in different models for small private institutions than those we traditionally associate with them.

Whether developed intentionally and over time or adapted quickly and by necessity, enough new approaches have now been developed and implemented to categorize the options into a taxonomy of small colleges and universities. This book explores those models in some depth, with institutional examples, to evaluate which approach may be more effective for a particular environment or campus. A deeper understanding of the models can help inform decision-making and institutional change for any independent college or university.

A Taxonomy of Small Colleges and Universities

A review of the landscape reveals a possible taxonomy of five emerging business and educational models for small private colleges and universities. Figure 3.1 provides a visual framework for understanding this taxonomy.

The first model is the most conventional, and the one where many small private institutions began: the traditional model. This is the vision most people still have of the small private college: bucolic, residential, focused on undergraduate education in the liberal arts and sciences. Students usually attend full time, rarely work outside campus, and typically graduate in four years. They enjoy the educational and artistic offerings of the campus, including a rigorous, high-touch classroom experience; an outstanding library; art galleries; performance spaces featuring theater, dance, and music; and a robust cocurricular life supported by an active student affairs office. The ideal of these institutions was once famously depicted by Amherst alumnus and former United States president James Garfield, who is attributed with the aphorism, "The ideal college is Mark Hopkins on one end of a log and a student on the other" (Rudolph, 1965).

This model contains the roots of most small colleges and universities in the nation. A core curriculum built on classic texts, close reading, critical analysis, rigorous pedagogy, and effective writing was once the common domain of small colleges. Many also began with libraries, museums, and

Figure 3.1. Contemporary models of innovation in higher education.

Integrated Model
Maintain liberal arts core and residential experience. Professional programs and graduate programs added to strengthen student recruitment and expand market.

Distinctive Program Model
Establish common student experience that is both curricular and cocurricular to enhance quality, recruitment, and retention. Maintain core liberal arts.

Traditional Model
Undergraduate, residential, liberal arts–based curriculum. Originally included faith-based and values-based institutions. Today, most that remain are wealthy with recruitment based on institutional quality and reputation.

Expansion Model
May or may not retain liberal arts commitment, focus on high-demand programs, usually in professional or graduate programs.

Distributed Model
Extensive enrollment in branch campuses and online programs to capture additional students. Modest or nonexistent liberal arts core and residential campus.

Marcy (2017a).

performing arts spaces at the heart of the campus. Although idealized as the purest of educational models (especially by graduates of such institutions), a truly robust traditional model is a challenge to maintain on either an educational or a financial level.

As a result, today the pure traditional model tends to be the domain of the well funded and well established—of the elite. Institutions with significant fiscal capacity and strong reputations have the resources to maintain and even strengthen their traditional approach in the face of the headwinds of changing demographics, shifting market demand, and a challenging economic environment. However, as we shall see, even these institutions are not static and are adapting to an environment that is changing in profound and irretrievable ways.

Given the ubiquity of the image of the small private liberal arts college, it is interesting—and important—to recognize how many small private colleges are no longer aligned with the traditional model. Many institutions have moved to other approaches, some of which continue to embrace their history in the traditional model and some of which explicitly move away from it. It is particularly valuable to understand in some depth the new paths they have taken, why they have adopted different approaches, and the results of those efforts.

Thus, while the traditional model may hold the history of most small colleges and universities, it is no longer the most common approach to education at these institutions. The more typical educational approach for independent colleges and universities is the integrated model, so named because it integrates the liberal arts with professional programs and also adds graduate programs tied to its undergraduate strengths.

This approach became more prevalent in the final decades of the twentieth century. At the time, many campuses, especially those lacking either a national reputation or significant resources, found it difficult to remain viable while staying fully in the traditional model. They began adding new programs that could diversify their academic offerings and expand the reach of the institution. These campuses were usually struggling with constrained resources and enrollment concerns and searching for ways to strengthen both, while maintaining fidelity to their liberal arts roots. Because many of these campuses were (and remain) strongly regional in focus, they also developed additional programs that had particular attraction in their service area.

Colleges in the integrated model maintain a liberal arts core and general education curriculum. The integrated model differs significantly from the traditional model, however, in the breadth and reach of its offerings. In addition to the liberal arts, these institutions provide a number of preprofessional, professional, and graduate programs. Such additions have nearly always been strategies to stabilize or grow enrollment in response to a flagging market for the traditional core, or in response to regional needs.

A few decades ago programs were often added in teacher education, business, or law. Today, new programs at both the undergraduate and graduate level are frequently added in the health sciences and in emerging technology fields such as data analytics, cybersecurity, and computer science. In recent years the reliance on graduate programs has also grown. A steadily rising financial aid discount rate has led to a stubborn stagnation in undergraduate net tuition revenue, and graduate programs have often offered more reliable growth in net tuition.

The most educationally compelling institutions in the integrated model are those that effectively integrate the liberal arts and the professions and do so not just in name, but in practice. These campuses are able to provide students with the benefits of a strong liberal arts education regardless of major and also prepare students for professions beyond the academy.

However, in recent years the more comprehensive approach of the integrated model has often faced serious challenges. So many small colleges and universities have adopted this approach that it is sometimes hard to distinguish one from the other. And it turns out the continual addition of new professional and preprofessional programs (as well as new buildings and faculty) is not necessarily sustainable in the face of the emerging realities of the twenty-first century. This has led a number of small colleges and universities to seek alternative models to make their institutions more sustainable.

One of these alternatives is the third model in the taxonomy: the distinctive program model. This model is somewhat less prevalent but has recently gained considerable currency. In this model, the small college or university builds its programs, as well as its institutional identity, around a common educational experience. By doing so, the campus seeks to answer the question: What is distinctive about this institution? More than a common academic core, this model is defined by a common student experience in which all programs, regardless of discipline, in and beyond the classroom, are aligned to support a common student learning process—sometimes referred to as a guided pathway. For example, all students may be required to study abroad as part of their degree requirements, or every program may have to provide evidence of engaged learning, student research, or leadership attainment.

The distinctive program approach involves more than the notion of moving from teaching to learning that was championed in the late 1990s (Barr & Tagg, 1995). That approach provided valuable insight into the ways we were supporting (or failing to support) student classroom learning and concentrated on changes to pedagogy. The distinctive program model moves beyond the pedagogical and requires a major reconceptualization of the institution by focusing on student learning experiences and outcomes across the campus and throughout students' time at the institution.

The distinctive program campus is different from institutions that develop a niche market based on a specific academic emphasis, such as infusing environmental sustainability throughout the curriculum. The distinctive program model is committed to infusing best practices for student success without regard to academic program and translates across a multitude of disciplines, in and out of the classroom.

It can be difficult to translate a common set of activities across disciplinary silos. It can also be difficult to implement this approach because most campuses are accustomed to treating any new programs as additions, not as something ubiquitous and integrated throughout the institution. The challenge is especially acute at institutions that have a broad mix of liberal arts, sciences, professional, and graduate programs—institutions where it is easier to distinguish what separates academic programs than what unites them.

The distinctive program model has the potential to evolve from either the traditional model or the integrated model. It builds on the best outcomes of liberal education while making room for programs beyond the liberal arts. Lori Varlotta (2018), president of Hiram College, makes a strong case for this vision of the "new liberal arts." This approach is compelling because it holds considerable promise for building a student experience based on high-impact practices, because it is responsive to changing student demographics, and because it evolves directly from the natural strengths of small colleges. By focusing the educational model on student learning and success, rather than program or disciplinary offerings, the campus can define itself by the quality of the overall student educational experience and student outcomes. As the profile of students becomes more diverse in all ways—ethnically complex, increasingly first-generation college, more frequently from lower socioeconomic backgrounds—the distinctive program model embraces emerging knowledge about student success to adapt the campus to this changing student profile. This model is in contrast to defining the campus by a few outstanding programs or by focusing solely on evolving disciplinary offerings that are market-driven. The distinctive program model allows a campus to identify and elevate its inherent strengths based on student learning, while still adapting to a changed external environment.

Another alternative that some independent colleges and universities have developed is the expansion model. The expansion model is a more business-oriented model and is fundamentally market driven. It is being adopted with increasing frequency by campuses seeking to address the challenges of shifting demographics and flatlining net tuition revenue. In the expansion model, the campus explicitly responds to market trends, often with some alacrity. While the integrated model is committed to the integration of the liberal arts and professional programs, the expansion model is less concerned with integration and may or may not retain a grounding in the liberal arts.

The expansion model responds to enrollment and fiscal challenges by both offering new academic programs and expanding existing programs. Often the expansion model is adopted by small colleges and universities that once would have been considered part of the integrated model and are ready to embrace a more entrepreneurial and aggressive approach.

The successful expansion model campus conducts thorough market research to understand current and ongoing demand for programs. It also fully evaluates the cost, in time and infrastructure, to build high-demand programs, in order to understand the window for return on investment. For example, to increase total institutional enrollment, a campus may admit increasing numbers of students in programs such as nursing or build new programs in high-demand majors such as computer science. Such programs require significant infrastructure and technology support. In addition, hiring and retaining well-qualified faculty is quite competitive in these fields and, thus, expensive. Specialized accreditation may be required for the program to effectively place students after graduation. Thus, even high-demand additions may or may not be sustainable and may or may not add to the financial viability of the campus. The effective expansion model institution is sophisticated in both its advance research and its ongoing implementation of new programs to ensure they are strong and enduring investments for the campus.

Most expansion model institutions are diversified in not only their academic program offerings but also their mode of educational delivery. Because they are committed to responding to student demand, they will offer online and hybrid programs to more readily meet the needs of students who are working, have families, or need a more flexible approach to their education. While many expansion model campuses have an on-campus student population that is regional, their online programs may considerably expand the reach of the institution, along with expanding enrollment. As is the case in adding new programs, the successful expansion model campus must carefully consider the cost and time to delivery of new online or hybrid programs, as well as the investment in faculty and staff professional development needed to make the programs successful and of quality.

Because of its orientation to market needs, campus facilities in the expansion model are also designed to align with areas of greatest demand. For long-established institutions originally grounded in the liberal arts, this may mean a shift in investment from the old physical spaces dedicated to, for example, the visual and performing arts toward more spaces dedicated to technology or specialized equipment and laboratories.

Unlike the traditional or the integrated model, the expansion model does not retain a strong fealty to the liberal arts beyond, perhaps, some general education requirements. Unlike the distinctive program model, it does not seek to create a common integrated student learning experience. Instead, the expansion model focuses on building a strong and visible reputation in areas of growing demand.

And finally, the fifth model for small colleges and universities is the distributed university model. The distributed model employs nearly all the strategies for change outlined at the beginning of this chapter: adding new locations, adding new programs, changing educational delivery modalities, and adjusting the business model. In the distributed model, the overall approach is nimble and highly entrepreneurial. Like the expansion model, it is also explicitly driven by emerging markets. But in the distributed model, there is less focus on adding programs to the home campus and more focus on extending the scale and reach of the institution, distributing its educational offerings across a wide geographical range.

This educational distribution is established by using new educational technologies and robust data analytics. Many programs are offered online or in a limited-residency format. Branch campuses and educational centers provide localized student support and help the campus reach new markets. The core infrastructure and back-office services are centralized and automated whenever feasible, in order to manage cost while building revenue through increasing enrollment.

The distributed model campus usually offers asynchronous learning and program launch times, recognizing that many students, especially working adults, cannot easily adapt to a traditional academic calendar. There is often a significant focus on the student as consumer, with a concomitant dedication to customer service. The successful distributed model campus thus makes significant investments in sophisticated learning management systems and in providing timely responses to student inquiries.

Because of the range of program offerings and educational delivery modalities, the distributed model campus often adopts a different approach to pricing than the usual high-tuition, high-financial-aid paradigm seen at most independent colleges and universities. Depending on the program, the campus may tie price to each specific course or offer a cost per credit hour and not have a general tuition rate across the institution. This financing approach recognizes that many of the students likely to enroll in their programs will be part time and will seek to build sufficient credentials for graduation over a longer period of time than the usual place-based model of education.

The distributed model institution seeks additional student markets that operate separately from the typical core undergraduate educational model. Depending on the level of growth in these new programs, they may come to define the institution, while the old undergraduate residential core operates somewhat independently, often funded by these new efforts. Sometimes the original residential undergraduate campus even ceases to exist.

The Taxonomy in Context

These five approaches are not linear, nor are they fully discrete. As small colleges and universities have evolved, most tend to use primarily one approach, while they may borrow a few ideas or tools from others. All too often these changes have not evolved from an integrated, institution-wide planning process but from the accumulation of short-term changes implemented with urgency in reaction to fiscal difficulties, enrollment needs, and emerging student markets. For example, a campus grounded in the liberal arts may find that, through the addition of high-demand programs and elimination of programs with less enrollment, it has lost its connection to liberal education.

Less frequently (but much preferred) is when campus evolution involves a planned integrative process where the institution self-consciously moves from one approach to another. This book is designed to help campuses develop a more integrated and planned pathway to address the fundamental challenges facing most institutions by outlining the taxonomy and considering the inherent strengths, challenges, and assumptions behind each path.

The taxonomy is a conceptual framework developed to create a deeper understanding of the different institutional models that have evolved over the last few decades. Within this overview are profound implications for institutional change and viability, as these institutions face the stresses and strains of a dramatically changed environment. Often the process of institutional change involves a move from one approach to another; indeed, evaluation of the relevance of different models is an important step to moving an institution to viability.

There is not one best, or preferred, model from either an educational or a financial standpoint. Not all five models align with specific institutional missions, and not all provide a stable fiscal path forward for all campuses. Their potential effectiveness varies based on the history, strengths, location, and leadership of a given campus. To bring about institutional viability, it is important for boards and leaders of small colleges and universities to understand the external environment; the emerging national and regional landscape; and their own institutional strengths, weaknesses, and position. This understanding allows campus leaders to evaluate the emerging small college models from an institutional perspective and to consider the strategic decisions necessary to succeed with a given approach.

A Continuum of Change

These five models capture the emerging educational and business approaches of most small private colleges and universities in the nation. Some campuses have adopted a specific model with considerable foresight and intention. Others are in a particular model by default, through the accretion of reactive decisions over multiple years.

The models are best understood not as independent, free-standing cells, but as a continuum of change. The continuum represents the degree of change usually required to adopt a particular approach, from moderate tweaking to significant adaptation to transformational. It also represents the degree of movement away from the traditional model, where many institutions began. Finally, the continuum captures the reality that, while institutions are *primarily* in one model, they may not be *exclusively* in a single model and may adopt some strategies from across the spectrum. They may also move from one model to another over time, through a planned (or unplanned) attempt to resolve financial concerns.

In the present environment, few small colleges are simply static in their approach to education. The continuum illustrated in Figure 3.2 captures a sense of this dynamism, as well as the degree of change being undertaken using different models. Many of the most elite and well-subsidized institutions are adopting new programs and more explicitly tying their liberal education to career opportunities, so even the traditional model is not static. Their adjustment may seem modest compared to others in the continuum but may still be dramatic for the campus itself. Campuses using the distinctive program model are likely undertaking substantial change to their educational approach in order to respond to changing students and address fiscal realities. The three cells on the left of the continuum—traditional, integrated, and distinctive program—all represent change within the historical paradigm of small colleges and universities. They retain a liberal arts core even as they adapt. They are also still highly focused on the traditional-age student.

Figure 3.2. Continuum of change.

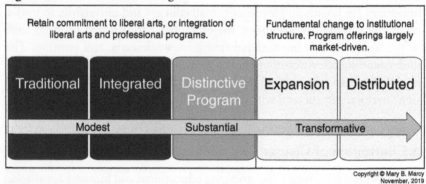

Institutions undertaking change toward the expansion or distributed model are undergoing a more fundamental change. These two right-hand cells represent comprehensive and transformational change; the campus, and even its mission, may look entirely different at the end of this transformation than it did at the beginning. Students may be older, more commuter and part-time, and the range of educational offerings may be far from the liberal arts core. The most successful ensure a responsiveness to student success that builds on the best aspects of small colleges and universities.

Fortunately, these models are not entirely new; small colleges and universities have been adapting to the challenging environment for some time. While the landscape is now shifting rapidly, enough campuses have strategically pursued these approaches over the last decade so that we can describe them in some depth, and we can usefully evaluate their progress. They are accompanied by a set of educational and financial outcomes that are instructive in understanding the promise and the challenge of each approach.

Which models are the most educationally effective for students? Which hold the most promise for serving our larger society? Which are the most financially viable for the long term? Which models secure the power and legacy of traditional higher education? The answers to these questions vary by type of institution, profile of students, region of the country, and timing of implementation. A closer look at the models, with institutional examples, will help us understand the inherent opportunities and challenges in each.

While too many institutions have stumbled into one or another of these models because of fiscal strain or shifts in leadership focus, it is much more desirable—and is likely becoming essential—that campuses become highly strategic as they choose a response to the challenging landscape. Most campuses do not have the luxury of trying multiple approaches to "see what sticks." Fewer can afford multiple false starts. It seems clear that consciously selecting a model, rather than simply offering a collection of programs that evolved from short-term decisions, provides a more promising future for our small colleges and universities.

Such a strategic approach allows an institution to develop data-driven targets for change while continuing to adapt to a very dynamic environment. Clear strategy and aligned data allow for midcourse adjustments even as the campus pursues a larger vision derived from an analysis of the likeliest route to success.

The next series of chapters will explore each model in turn. Each chapter will consider the strengths, weaknesses, and risks inherent in each approach. The conclusion of each chapter will provide institutional profiles of campuses that have successfully adopted that particular model, so that other institutions can learn from the experience of early adopters and leading examples in each area. The profiles will highlight both the content and the process used to realize success in each model.

4

UNDERSTANDING THE
TRADITIONAL MODEL

The traditional model of small colleges and universities is the one still most closely associated with independent higher education. These campuses usually have a long history and tradition of delivering liberal arts education in a residential setting. The traditional approach is the one initially adopted by most small private institutions. More recently, new institutions have focused on skills currently in demand or more definitively tied to the job market. And, as we will see, many campuses that began in the traditional model have embraced other approaches in order to remain viable. This leaves a fairly elite and specific set of institutions in the pure traditional model. However, although many are relatively wealthy and selective, even these institutions are adapting to the demographic and other challenges facing independent colleges across the nation.

In the traditional model, campuses are focused almost exclusively on the undergraduate liberal arts and sciences, often with their own institutional vision for liberal education. Both the general education curriculum and the disciplinary offerings of campuses in the traditional model are dedicated to liberal education, although the specific range of programs and required courses varies by institution. They may have a central "great books" core or be focused on the liberal arts and sciences with a strong social science program. Historically, these distinctions among traditional institutions have been important, as they have created particular niches for individual campuses and led to thoughtful exploration and debate about the humanities, liberal education, and our democracy. For example, arguments about the canon and the great books have emerged as institutions have grappled with their own legacy and with the changing profile of their students. As our reliance on technology has grown, these campuses have brought forward thoughtful discussions about the role of reflective learning in a society that offers nearly infinite opportunities for distraction.

While such debates about the nature of liberal education are important, even essential, they are not enough to help chart a path to the future for most campuses. And for the purposes of this analysis, what unites traditional liberal arts institutions is more important than what separates them. What they have in common, of course, is liberal education. As defined by the institution, liberal education is at the heart of all educational work. Highly residential, these institutions seek to provide a comprehensive student experience, with a strong library, traditional (if technologically well-equipped) classrooms, a low student-to-faculty ratio, a robust cocurricular life, and a student union that serves at the intersection of the academic and residential programs.

This model contains the roots of most small colleges in the nation, particularly those founded in the 1800s and those in the Midwest and East. A core curriculum built on classic texts, close reading, critical analysis, rigorous pedagogy, and effective writing was once the common domain of most small colleges. This work traditionally happened in small classes led by full-time, tenure-line faculty. Most also began with libraries, museums, and performing arts spaces at the heart of the campus.

While most small colleges began with these common roots, today the pure traditional model is not the most typical approach for small colleges. It tends to be the domain of the more elite and aspiring-to-elite institutions. These campuses practice their vision of liberal education in the midst of the headwinds of changing demographics, shifting market demand, and a challenging economic environment. As a result, most of those campuses that remain in the traditional model have considerable resources and/or reputational advantage, enough to maintain a picturesque campus and retain the liberal arts at the center of their curricular and programmatic identities. They give less attention to immediate, shifting market forces and focus instead on enduring questions of thought, democratic engagement, and meaning.

To be sure, there are distinctions among the institutions within the traditional model, particularly in their notion of what constitutes a liberal education. But their fidelity to the liberal arts and their residential nature distinguish them. Admission to these institutions is often highly competitive due to their perceived quality, reputation, resources, and strong alumni network. Students who attend these elite institutions can be assured of a comprehensive experience that will expose them to some of the best intellectual and cocurricular opportunities available in higher education. At the same time, students can also expect to receive the personalized attention that is the domain of all small colleges, albeit in more rarefied surroundings, and with a more highly credentialed faculty than most.

Defining Features of the Traditional Model

There are several essential characteristics of the traditional model. The most significant is the centrality of the liberal arts and sciences to the academic work of the campus. While most institutions that offer the bachelor's degree retain a general education core that draws strongly from the liberal arts, traditional campuses are focused almost entirely on liberal education throughout their curriculum. This means that the vast majority of degree programs are in the liberal arts and sciences. In addition, many campuses have developed sophisticated general-education programs that are nuanced and institution specific, built around a particular notion of liberal education. For example, Bard College has a core curriculum that begins with "Language and Thinking," while St. John's College has a Great Books core (Bard College, 2019; St. John's College, 2019). Other campuses in the traditional model may alter the conventional academic calendar or emphasize one particular aspect of liberal education; for example, Colorado College offers a Block Plan—an intensive one-course-at-a-time calendar (Colorado College, 2019). Kalamazoo College has the K Plan, with a specific emphasis on personalized curriculum development and internationalization (Kalamazoo College, 2019).

Colleges in the traditional model are also heavily focused on undergraduate education. Indeed, many higher education leaders believe that "liberal arts colleges represent the ideal for undergraduate education" (Chopp, 2013). These campuses offer few, if any, graduate degrees. If they do offer graduate programs, those programs are usually in traditional liberal arts disciplines and complementary to the undergraduate program, rather than usurping that educational focus.

The majority of faculty in the traditional model are tenure-line faculty with terminal degrees and often quite distinguished records in their disciplines. Faculty on these campuses teach predominantly at the undergraduate level in small, seminar-style classes, and their teaching and research are often well-integrated. As a result, students frequently have the opportunity to conduct research at an early stage in their education, one of the many attractions and educational distinctions of the traditional model.

Traditional liberal arts colleges are also highly residential. First-year and often second-year students are usually required to live on campus, and the majority of students of all class levels live in housing on or near the campus itself. This residential tenor also means the campuses have a robust set of events and activities designed to nurture the college as a learning community. They typically develop substantial cocurricular programs that embrace the campus ethos and mission. For example, Reed College's Honor Principle is a "noncodified philosophy of behavior" that "extends beyond the classroom" (Reed College, 2019), and Earlham's program of "Principles and Practices" draws from its Quaker roots to integrate in- and out-of-classroom activity and bring students fully into the life of the college (Earlham College, 2019).

Adding to the residential experience is a robust set of facilities and programs. Study abroad experiences are common and often have high participation. Service-learning and civic engagement work are frequently a centerpiece of campus culture. Campus cocurricular programming is usually quite active, with many options for student engagement.

Traditional campuses are also usually home to art museums, often with extensive historic collections created at the founding of the college, that bring contemporary exhibits to the campus and showcase student and faculty work. The campus will likely have a performing arts venue that provides similar space for music, theater, and dance, ensuring that the creative and performing arts are an important component of campus life.

Inherent Strengths of the Traditional Model

The strengths of the traditional model are apparent. When well supported and effectively implemented, this approach provides a rigorous, personalized education of exceptional quality. The low student-to-faculty ratio and commitment to undergraduate liberal arts education mean that students are both nurtured and challenged. The focus on liberal education invites students to question, reflect, find their own voice, and engage in thoughtful ways with their community and with society. Because the focus is almost entirely on undergraduate education, the standards for academic quality are constantly discussed and usually quite high.

Similarly, the traditional model offers an enviable residential experience for students, with exposure to a culturally rich array of programs and events. Whether students are majoring in the arts or not, they often have access to a wide range of cultural experiences, both through campus collections and through visiting artists, speakers, performers, and activities. Because the campuses are modest in size, students not only see these performances but have unusually close access.

The campuses are small enough to create intentional communities, ones that nurture students' intellects and talents while inculcating a sense of campus values and mores. The robust residential community often means that institutional values around personal behavior, social responsibility, and community engagement are embedded in the student experience. If done with care and academic rigor, there is little doubt the traditional model delivers an education, and a personal experience, of exceptional quality.

Inherent Challenges of the Traditional Model

Just as the strengths of the traditional model are evident, so too are the challenges. A high-quality education delivered through the traditional model is expensive, even by contemporary higher education standards. The services, facilities, faculty, and staff support required to maintain and curate historic buildings, large collections, and extensive grounds are significant. And maintaining a low student-to-faculty ratio while supporting extensive faculty development and maintaining a modest faculty course load can be challenging for any institution.

Along with the challenge of cost is—for all but the most high-profile campuses—the challenge of student recruitment. As higher education is increasingly viewed by society as a personal investment and one focused on career trajectory, there has been commensurate pressure on liberal arts colleges to not merely provide a high-quality education, but one that is perceived to be relevant to the job market. This is a fundamental shift from education for its own sake; from education for a democratic society; or from education based on the goals of critical thinking, analysis, close reading, and an appreciation for the arts. Indeed, one of the major concerns of losing more institutions from the traditional model is the potential erosion of these profound purposes of higher education.

The fact is that the outcomes of a liberal education and career success are not in conflict. Indeed, research indicates that a liberal education leads to significant professional opportunity as well as personal benefits (Hill & Davidson Pisacreta, 2019). But this is a fact that is not well known, especially by the growing population of first-generation college students—nor is it a fact highlighted by the media's coverage of higher education.

Liberal education is perceived by many to be a luxury for the privileged, rather than a practical education that will provide a return on the investment in a college education. As more traditional age students are first generation college students, and as the pressure to show the outcomes (usually defined as employment soon after graduation) of higher education grows, so too do the challenges of recruiting students to attend liberal arts colleges. For those institutions with high status, the elite nature of the institution counters concerns about the job market. For many other liberal arts institutions that are of high quality but not perceived to be among the elite, the student recruitment challenge is real and growing.

Finally, one of the major issues facing many colleges in the traditional model is the challenge of change itself. Because these campuses have spent years—usually decades, if not longer—crafting an institution-specific notion of liberal education, it can be very difficult to make any fundamental change to that education. In some cases, change of any sort is not needed. But in many, it is not only needed but essential. Even well-resourced institutions will be affected by shifts in student demographics and changing expectations for higher education. As we will see, some are finding thoughtful ways to uphold their commitment to liberal education while providing greater opportunity and while tying education more clearly to life and career paths. Such change is very difficult at a campus that has not needed to discuss the outcomes or the bottom line in the past. Effective leadership and a strong vision can help these campuses respond to the changing environment in thoughtful ways.

Contemporary Examples of the Traditional Model

While the traditional model tends to be associated today with more financially robust and reputationally strong institutions, most of these campuses are still conscious of the larger forces facing small private colleges and universities. Their process for responding to these forces is nuanced and involves strategic additions or adjustment to the core liberal arts program, rather than overshadowing or replacing this core. The ways in which they are adapting can be seen in more detail in the accompanying profiles, which feature two institutions that are firmly within the traditional model, albeit located in very different regions of the country: Whitman College and Colgate University.

Whitman College, located in Walla Walla, Washington, became a four-year, degree-granting institution in 1883. Long recognized as a campus dedicated to rigorous education, in 1913 Whitman was the first institution in the country to require undergraduates to complete comprehensive examinations in their fields. A member of the selective "Northwest Five" consortium of colleges, Whitman is consistently listed as one of the top 50 liberal arts colleges in the country. Its website states that Whitman "provides a rigorous liberal arts education of the highest quality," and its 1,500 undergraduate students choose from 49 departmental majors (Whitman College, 2019).

Colgate University, located on the other side of the United States, was founded in 1819 in Hamilton, New York, and has long held a place in the upper echelon of American higher education. Larger than many liberal arts colleges, Colgate has nearly 3,000 undergraduate students and offers 56 majors and 48 minors. An essential aspect of a Colgate education is the core curriculum that has been in place since the early part of the twentieth century. The core addresses issues that reach beyond a single discipline and is a defining feature of the Colgate experience for both students and alumni (Colgate University, n.d.c).

It is instructive to see both the commonalities and the differences in the ways in which these two traditional institutions are adapting for the future. Both have developed, or are in the process of developing, a new strategic vision that evolved from new presidential leadership and a desire to adapt to changing student needs. Ongoing listening tours and evaluation of institutional data informed the development of the plans. This process takes time, and because the campuses have considerable resources and reputation, they have had the luxury of time to evolve a comprehensive, fully engaged process. And it is notable that these new strategic visions both include an unequivocal ongoing commitment to—what one of the presidents referred to as "doubling down on"—the liberal arts (Casey, 2018).

Both Colgate and Whitman are funding their new plans through a combination of philanthropy and focused endowment draws. Because they have significant existing resources, as well as an enviable philanthropic base, they are able to fund most new initiatives as additions, rather than redirecting funds from their existing campus programs and activities. This distinction is important, as we will see later in the book when evaluating other models of change adopted by less wealthy institutions.

Whitman and Colgate are also consciously developing new visions that assume a changing student demographic. In Colgate's case, this means a new, highly visible career services facility and program located in the heart of campus. For Whitman, it has meant a sharply heightened commitment to access and diversity, and to helping students with "life after Whitman."

The accompanying profiles provide a more in-depth look at the changes each campus is undertaking as they respond to the shifting landscape.

PROFILE OF A TRADITIONAL MODEL INSTITUTION: WHITMAN COLLEGE

Field research and draft compilation of this campus profile conducted by Bryce William Ervin while an EdM student at the Harvard Graduate School of Education

Brief Institutional History

Whitman College, located in Walla Walla, Washington, became a four-year, degree-granting college in 1883 after the state legislature issued a new charter (Whitman College, n.d.e). Since then, Whitman College has prided itself on its independent, nonsectarian nature, small size, and intimate faculty-student connection. This ideal is embodied in Whitman's mission statement and reflects the traditional, liberal arts model of the institution, emphasizing a "supportive scholarly community that prioritizes student learning within and beyond our classrooms" (Whitman College, n.d.g).

Core Identity

With a recent enrollment of 1,475 students, Whitman exemplifies the classification of a small, residential, liberal arts college. The college offers 48 majors and 34 minors with the recent addition of computer science (Whitman College, n.d.a). Additionally, students have the opportunity to pursue combined plans or craft a new area of interdisciplinary study. A 9:1 student-to-faculty ratio provides students the opportunity to work closely with professors and allows for the rich learning experience undergraduates find in small class sizes. Whitman's core curriculum is called the General Studies Program. It falls along traditional academic lines by requiring a first-year experience course and 6 distribution requirements covering a wide breadth of different disciplines ranging from quantitative analysis to cultural pluralism (Whitman College, n.d.b, n.d.d).

Whitman students typically reside in on-campus housing for their first 2 years. The college itself has an easily walkable, quiet, tree-filled campus, with nearly 30 sculptures and works of art by famous artists dotting the quads, lawns, and walkways.

Recent Developments

Since the early 1990s, Whitman has experienced a significant increase in the quality of its student profile, with a clear increase in graduation rates and average incoming high school GPAs and SAT scores (Whitman College Institutional Research, personal communication, 2019). Introducing merit aid helped to elevate academic strength, retention, and the graduation of students from the college. During this time, Whitman's identity in the region and country became further established. This change enabled Whitman's growth from a largely regional institution to a more nationally recognized one, attracting students from a much broader geographic territory (P. Harvey, personal interview, January 16, 2019).

Faculty, similarly, have become more professionally active in their scholarship, which has enabled students to assist in research and to leverage close faculty relationships to pursue their own research. These compounding effects have increased the caliber of the Whitman faculty as a whole and, in conjunction with a strong sabbatical program, enabled the college to better attract, retain, and provide continuing professional development for faculty (P. Harvey, personal interview, January 16, 2019).

In the last few years, Whitman reallocated funds within existing budgets, primarily to support financial aid efforts. Today, Whitman's endowment is more than $550 million.

Fit Within Models

Within the framework of small independent colleges outlined in this book, Whitman is firmly traditional. The college strongly holds to the value of a liberal arts education, maintaining its small size, emphasizing the connection between students and professors, and fostering a sense of community among students through residential offerings and student clubs and organizations. Whitman grants bachelor of arts degrees and does not have any graduate or specialized schools or online programs. The majority of Whitman's first-year students enter directly after graduating from high school.

The New Strategic Plan

While Whitman fits comfortably within the traditional model, the college is still consciously adapting to changes in student demographics and other issues facing higher education. The process of embracing the liberal arts while changing to meet contemporary demands is illustrated by the leadership of Whitman's relatively new president.

President Kathleen Murray began her presidency in 2015. As a central element of her leadership, the board of trustees and President Murray laid the groundwork for a new strategic plan for Whitman, one that would honor the campus's history while responding to new and emerging realities. The move toward a formal strategic plan developed from an existing context of stability and strength, characterized by Whitman's solid market presence, effective financial management, and high-quality academic programs. At the same time, Whitman's leadership recognized that proactive change would be necessary to maintain the essential values of the institution and to better communicate the importance of a traditional liberal arts education in a changing, and challenging, higher education environment. This perspective is clearly conveyed by the goal of the plan, which is "to develop bold aspirations for Whitman's future, while building on the college's historic strengths" (Whitman College, 2017).

In 2015, prior to starting the strategic planning process, President Murray spent much of her first year connecting with the Whitman community, as well as learning more fully the values that define the college. In an interview, President Murray emphasized that the planning process would be based on Whitman's culture (personal interview, November 20, 2018). This intentionality, with a focus on culture and values, was confirmed and supported by senior staff (J. Bogley, N. Christopherson, K. Joshua, personal interviews, January 16, 2019). The college began developing a comprehensive strategic planning initiative the following in, year 2016. The planning process is driven in part by marketplace expectations and also by how various involved constituencies believe Whitman should respond to a changing higher education environment.

Metrics and Data

The new planning process has incorporated the use of metrics and data-informed decision-making. This may not seem revolutionary, but for Whitman, it has been a departure from past experiences. While faculty and others in a traditional liberal arts institution may resist the use of metrics and market forces, staff noted in interviews that the strategic planning committee listened to concerns and requests more than in previous planning efforts, while still committing to a data-informed process (J. Bogley, N. Christopherson, K. Joshua, personal interviews, January 16, 2019).

Meanwhile new members of the board of trustees have been advocating for greater use of metrics to assess success at Whitman (N. Serrurier, personal interview, January 16, 2019). Accreditors also are encouraging more robust assessment for student learning. Whitman's Office of Institutional Research has been growing in both size and utilization on campus and is helping advise new data-informed decision making processes. Campus leaders acknowledge the importance of using data to make decisions in the current market, even if use of those data has the potential to run against traditional academic cultural mores.

At the same time, leadership has retained a determination to remain true to the Whitman community and understand how different key groups envision the institution. Whitman's leadership consistently focused on the strategic plan building on the college's core values. The chair of the board of trustees, Nancy Serrurier, highlighted the importance of the strength of Whitman's community. For one aspect of metric use, both Chair Serrurier and President Murray emphasized the importance of alumni data and surveys as a means to understand essential history, help inform change, and better prepare students for the world (personal interviews, January 16, 2019). The Whitman community as a whole strongly reflects an unapologetic and enthusiastic celebration of the liberal arts, and while data and marketplace factors will be utilized in the process, the strategic plan will not alter this essential identity.

Structure of Planning Committee and Approach

The strategic planning committee was cochaired by President Murray, the vice chair of the board of trustees, and the chair of the faculty. The decision to have three cochairs was intentional, in an effort to model the shared governance of the college (K. Murray, personal interview, November 20, 2018). In addition to the three cochairs, the committee included faculty, staff, governing board members, and students. In a departure from previous plans, Whitman approached the current strategic plan development with intentional inclusivity, engaging the on-campus community and representatives of the broader Whitman community as priorities were identified. In early 2017, five strategic priorities began to emerge. President Murray then embarked on trips around the country to engage alums, donors, and parents and get their perspective and feedback on the developing priorities (K. Murray, personal interview, November 20, 2018).

Identifying and Focusing the Priorities

In August 2017, the committee proposed its finalized five high-level priorities to the board of trustees, and they were subsequently approved. The priorities are (a) increasing access and availability; (b) enhancing diversity, equity, and inclusion; (c) innovating the curriculum; (d) connecting to life after Whitman; and (e) celebrating our location. In interviews, senior staff explained that these five priorities illuminate key pillars that are important to the entire Whitman community (J. Bogley, N. Christopherson, K. Joshua, personal interviews, January 16, 2019). The strategic plan is a response to changing markets and external pressures, as well as part of the natural evolution of the institution. Defining the strategic priorities challenged the Whitman community to determine Whitman's existing strengths and to envision what the institution can and should be in the future (K. Murray, personal interview, November 20, 2018).

Indicative of this inclusive effort is the establishment of working groups for each of the five priorities. Each group, in line with shared governance, has faculty, staff, and student representation; each is chaired by a vice president in a relevant area. These groups are charged with developing implementation tactics for each priority. With each priority, serious consideration was given to what could be done without major financial investment. Elements of this low-hanging fruit are already in some stage of implementation.

As part of the process, each working group also identified high-cost, big-lift items. For example, the largest potential cost, as outlined by Vice President Peter Harvey, would be the capital needed to make Whitman a 100% residential campus (personal interview, January 16, 2019). The strategic planning committee elected to not immediately pursue 100% residency due to the substantial cost and the need to support other priorities, although it remains an aspirational goal. Financial aid is another major expense and is tied directly to increasing access and affordability, as well as enhancing diversity, equity, and inclusion. These initiatives, as President Murray observed, emphasize Whitman's goal of attracting a diverse population of students and providing structure and support to ensure all students feel included and treated equitably (personal interview, November 20, 2018). From these and other large-ticket aspirations, the strategic planning committee then generated three focused priority "buckets" to make implementation and fundraising manageable. The three focused priority areas decided by the strategic planning committee are (a) increasing access and affordability, (b) innovating the learning and living environment, and (c) connecting to life after Whitman.

The testing of these three main "bucket" areas extended beyond the campus community to include alumni, parents, and friends. With refined priorities, an additional round of gathering campus community input was conducted to confirm the strategic plan. With adequate buy-in, the revised approach was then approved by the board of trustees, and President Murray began the initial silent phase of a fundraising campaign.

Increasing Access and Affordability

Increasing access and affordability are essential to ensuring Whitman's visible presence in an increasingly challenging higher education marketplace. As President Murray noted, the kind of education that Whitman offers is unlikely to become more affordable in the future (personal interview, November 20, 2018). This, for President Murray and the board, means that access and affordability were a critical part of their work. With Whitman's shift toward merit aid in the early 1990s, there is now increasing pressure to fund financial aid at a higher level while maintaining the merit aid program (P. Harvey, personal interview, January 16, 2019). As outlined in the strategic plan, "Whitman's ultimate goal is to meet the full demonstrated financial need of all admitted students" (Whitman College, 2017). Senior administrators note that the challenges the college must address include attracting diverse student populations, who are increasingly interested in attending institutions in urban areas, and generating a sense of belonging and offering the support needed for this increasingly diverse student body (J. Bogley, N. Christopherson, K. Joshua, personal interviews, January 16, 2019). The high costs entailed in such a focused priority link to a fundraising campaign currently in development to support the strategic plan.

Innovating the Learning and Living Environment: Revising the Curriculum

Whitman faculty are engaging in curriculum revision with particular focus around the college's general education requirements. While the process of curriculum revision is time consuming, actual planning and revision has been operating quite quickly on a faculty timescale. Whitman's provost, Alzada Tipton, noted in an interview that the working group taking on this major effort is purposefully working on a relatively accelerated timeline and is looking to enact change in the near term: approximately 18 months from conception to presenting a plan to the board of trustees (personal interview, January 16, 2019).

As to what precipitated this change, Provost Tipton observed that faculty found that the language developed in the working groups related to the curriculum does not reflect the current curriculum (personal interview, January 16, 2019). Whitman's existing curriculum is quite traditional, with a classic set of distribution requirements and a required first-year shared course. Culturally, Whitman is an institution where the academic major has received much of the curricular focus, and general education has received less attention. With this initiative, Provost Tipton observed that the working group aims to elevate the general education curriculum to the same intellectually engaging experience that students receive through their majors (personal interview, January 16, 2019). Provost Tipton noted that the current requirements only begin to address the areas where faculty would like to see greater emphasis, such as transferable skills or core knowledge. In addition, faculty are interested in exploring the dispositions or habits of thought a liberal arts education might impart. Notably, in a move that reaches beyond the traditional liberal arts curricular model, Provost Tipton noted that faculty would like to see students design and integrate their own learning, rather than using a classic distribution model that is quite specific in its requirements. There are numerous challenges inherent in this process, with advising and support being principal concerns. Another critical element for tying the curriculum to the broader strategic plan is weaving diversity, equity, and inclusion initiatives into the curriculum and academic offerings (A. Tipton, personal interview, January 16, 2019).

Connecting to Life After Whitman

Connecting to life after Whitman synthesizes many of the priorities of the strategic plan. While the priority itself does emphasize connecting with alumni and charting a path post-Whitman, the essential components that bring students to this stage involve the entire campus and encompass the full undergraduate experience. President Murray, in her installation address, acknowledged Whitman's curriculum, cocurriculum, and varied student experiences but emphasized that "students have only one life at our college"—and that that life does not have a distinct delineation "between life in the classroom and beyond the classroom" (Murray, 2015). President Murray encouraged the college as a whole to "focus on what is best for student learning, [and] to help each student develop a personal narrative that makes sense of that learning and carries them into a lifetime of continued learning" (Murray, 2015).

As outlined in the strategic priorities, this developed narrative would integrate Whitman students experiences and passions in and out of the classroom; encourage them to think deeply about the connections between their work, program, and community engagement; and continue to develop that into their lives beyond the college (Whitman College, 2017). This would not only better enable students to synthesize, bring together, and get the most out of their experience but also enable them to "translate their liberal arts education into a meaningful and satisfying life path" (Murray, 2015). Generating this "compelling narrative for their future" is no small task, and President Murray emphasizes that it will take a college community effort to work together to support that student learning goal (Whitman College, 2017). One of the greatest contemporary challenges Whitman and other small liberal arts colleges face is communicating the value and importance of the kind of education they offer. All of the priorities define and recommit Whitman to what its community finds as its essential values. A critical piece of ensuring Whitman's continued relevance and strength in a tumultuous higher education environment is to empower students with the ability to effectively translate their experiences to a greater audience, and to lead successful, fulfilling lives.

Looking Forward

Whitman is in the midst of enacting its current strategic plan. The working groups and strategic planning committee have completed their objectives, and the ongoing work is being guided by the cabinet, which will appoint new working groups as needed. While the faculty completes its curricular work, ongoing testing for a capital campaign is underway. The strategic plan and implementation machinery is fully engaged in what has been an inclusive institutional planning process. Whitman's change may appear subtle to those on the outside. Even with full completion of the strategic plan it will remain a small liberal arts institution and retain the best elements of its culture and character, firmly in the traditional model. Internally, however, these changes are viewed along the lines of being substantial, transformative, and

Figure 4.1. Whitman College at a glance.

Endowment	$561 million
Student to Faculty Ratio	9:1
Enrollment	1,475
Four-Year Graduation Rate	80.8%
Six-Year Graduation Rate	87.4%
Key Elements of the Curriculum	48 majors Classic liberal arts curriculum General studies program consists of distribution requirements (six with defined learning outcomes) and a shared first-year experience, *Encounters*

Note: U.S. Department of Education 2019; Whitman College (n.d.a).

necessary (K. Murray, personal interview, November 20, 2018). They are the changes needed for even a well-endowed and highly regarded institution to adapt to the headwinds and changing environment for small colleges and universities.

PROFILE OF A TRADITIONAL MODEL INSTITUTION: COLGATE UNIVERSITY

Field research and draft compilation of this campus profile conducted by Bryce William Ervin while an EdM student at the Harvard Graduate School of Education

Brief Institutional History

Colgate's picturesque campus is nestled in the middle of tree-filled rolling hills in the small town of Hamilton, New York. With award-winning architecture, the campus is what many would imagine when asked to picture a classic institution of higher learning—though you may need to swap stark red brick for rough-hewn local stone offering a range of greys, blues, and warm earth tones. The initial charter for Colgate University was granted to the Baptist Education Society of New York in 1819. From the initial founding of the society, the group formed the Hamilton Literary and Theological Institution through integration of their seminary and the local school in Hamilton. Hamilton Literary and Theological Institution was renamed Madison University in 1846. In the 1880s there was a push from the Madison County community to rename the university Colgate, after William Colgate, one of the initial founders of the Baptist Education Society of New York. Interestingly, the Colgate family was not consulted prior to the renaming effort and "did not favor it, but . . . they 'assented rather than embarrass its advocates'" (Colgate University, n.d.e). The Colgate family had long been involved in the institution through financial support and leadership.

Core Identity and Fit With Models

Today, Colgate celebrates its "long sustained [and] profound commitment to the liberal arts" (Colgate University, 2018a). Though Colgate is a university (as it offers a master of arts in teaching), undergraduates pursuing a traditional liberal arts education and Bachelor of Arts degrees make up the majority of its student body (Colgate University, 2018b). Colgate's mission statement emphasizes that the "purpose of the university is to develop wise, thoughtful, critical thinkers and perceptive leaders . . . through residence in a community that values intellectual rigor and respects the complexity of human understanding" (Colgate University, 1993). Relative to similar liberal arts institutions, Colgate has a somewhat larger student population of nearly 3,000 and its athletics teams compete in NCAA Division I (Casey, 2018). Colgate was an early leader in prioritizing support for faculty research during the second half of the twentieth century (Casey, 2018). This emphasis resulted in a clear scholarly role for faculty, extensive physical plant infrastructure development, and the acquisition of new research grants.

Vision Statement

Colgate University's Third Century: A Vision Statement is a vision document written by Colgate's current president, Brian Casey (2018), who was inaugurated in 2016. In an interview, President Casey observed that the vision statement originated from conversations with alumni who were curious to know his perspective on the future of Colgate (personal interview, March 1, 2019). The intent of this initial statement is to capture the strengths and values of Colgate and to give focus to those areas that the university will prioritize in the next phase of its development, as outlined in the next strategic plan. President Casey's vision statement emphasizes four key elements that form Colgate's distinctive character. In addition, it outlines several intangible factors that define the university. Together, this framing of the institution also shapes its next steps in responding to a changing higher education landscape while retaining fidelity to its core identity.

The Four Key Elements

President Casey's vision emphasizes four key elements that define Colgate, and that he believes will also be essential to crafting the institution's future. Those four elements include an ongoing commitment to the liberal arts, continuing support for the core curriculum, an emphasis on international study, and a focus on the residential life of the university.

Commitment to the Liberal Arts

President Casey's vision statement includes an ongoing commitment to liberal education. Colgate's curriculum focuses on the core liberal arts ideals of developing "fundamental skills and habits of mind" and requires students to pursue study across core disciplines (Colgate University, n.d.c). Through rigorous study, Colgate students will develop skill sets including "critical inquiry, effective argumentation and communication, and creativity," which "remain hallmarks of a Colgate education" (Casey, 2018). The university offers 56 majors and 48 minors and organizes academic programs into four divisions: arts and humanities, social sciences, natural sciences and mathematics, and university studies.

Upholding the Core Curriculum

The university's core curriculum is unusual among Colgate's liberal arts peers, not least because it has been unchanged since the 1920s. It consists of five required courses that every student must take by the end of the sophomore year (Colgate University, n.d.c). These common academic experiences focus "on issues and topics that go beyond any single academic discipline" (Colgate University, 2018a) and include such titles as Legacies of the Ancient World, and Communities and Identities. Importantly, the core curriculum also acts as "a key touchstone for Colgate alumni" (Casey, 2018). It is an experience that develops bonds and fosters community among Colgate students.

Commitment to International Study

Colgate has been a longtime leader in encouraging students to pursue study away experiences. Seeking "exposure to different cultures and ideas has long been part of the Colgate experience" (Casey, 2018). The university now offers more than 100 study abroad opportunities in more than 50 countries.

The Residential Life of the University

The residential experience has been a core fixture in Colgate's history, and today the majority of students live on campus all four years (Colgate University, n.d.d). The great variety of housing options, subcommunities, and the Residential Commons[1] program form an essential foundation for a close-knit community valued by students and alumni. Embedded in Colgate's mission statement is the development of core skills and values through "residence in a community" (Colgate University, 1993).

Intangible Factors

President Casey also emphasizes intangible aspects of the university that are nonetheless central to its identity. He cites Colgate's size, energy, and sense of place in this category. Colgate's large size, in comparison to most liberal arts colleges, allows for opportunities that would otherwise be unavailable and when combined with the university's NCAA Division I status provides a "culture feel . . . more like Dartmouth College or Duke University" (Casey, 2018).

In concert with the university's size is the energy of engaged, passionate students, faculty, and staff. President Casey emphasizes that the intersection of size and energy enables opportunities for students to have deep and meaningful experiences both in and out of the classroom.

The final intangible factor is Colgate's sense of place. The campus itself is quite picturesque, with a location on the side of a hill surrounded by considerable open land. In the autumn, the whole area transitions from a lush green into vibrant fiery hues. For Colgate students and alums, the campus provides a "sense of place, . . . support[s] a sense of community, and serves as a powerful connection" (Casey, 2018).

Essentials for the Future

President Casey's "fundamentals for Colgate's future" provide a primary framework on which the university can build. These foundations include building and supporting a culture of intellectual rigor; attracting outstanding students; creating and nurturing a community marked by affection, ritual, and pride; and sustaining and improving a campus of striking beauty (Casey, 2018). There is a poetic consistency in the narrative that President Casey has developed that connects the key historical elements of Colgate, its essential intangibles that resonate with the contemporary community, and the future aspirations of a university with such a legacy. It is no surprise that President Casey's academic expertise is in "the history of American higher education and American intellectual history" (Colgate University, n.d.b).

New and Emerging Initiatives

While Colgate's next strategic plan is under development, it will grow—at least in part—out of *Colgate University's Third Century: A Vision Statement* (Casey, 2018). Given the strength of the university's position, President Casey noted that the future strategic plan will be a commitment to the liberal arts and a "doubling down" on Colgate's strengths (personal interview, March 1, 2019).

Colgate is approaching change adaptively, thoughtfully, and with no desire or need to pursue transformative or revolutionary action. The university has a firm presence in the higher education field and has strength in its offerings, students, faculty, financial stability, and alumni loyalty. The strategic planning process was based on many conversations within the Colgate community and planning committees and was somewhat less focused on data-driven processes.

Process and Approach

Rather than creating a new committee for planning, President Casey decided to leverage existing committees to take responsibility in the planning process. He also refocused and elevated an underutilized committee—the advisory and planning committee—to lead the process. This body of 20 people is responsible for receiving reports from other committees to bring together the new third century plan. The process of developing the plan took 2 years. Funding for the initiatives resulting from the plan will be provided by previous debt,[2] an endowment draw to launch a new campaign, and, ultimately, the proceeds from the new fundraising campaign. Colgate's ability to leverage debt without a particular project, simply to expand its position, is unusual in the current higher education landscape, and highlights the ability of wealthy institutions to "double down" on the liberal arts; conversely, it illustrates the challenges for less financially robust institutions and explains why other approaches, like those outlined in other models in this book, are being adopted.

There have also been several important process changes since President Casey's start at Colgate. First, as noted in an interview with the senior vice president for finance and administration, J.S. Hope, the board of trustees underwent governance restructuring (personal interview, March 12, 2019). Rather than the cumbersome qualities of formerly large committees, the board now has focused programmatic committees that provide the opportunity for greater engagement with, and commitment to, their work.

Second, President Casey used the expertise of outside marketing firms to better understand how external groups perceive the university, and to strengthen how Colgate tells its story. As Senior Vice President Hope observed, the results from this have been funneled into new initiatives in communications and admissions (personal interview, March 11, 2019).

Additionally, once the strategic planning process was underway, university finance staff were included as a partner. This inclusion was an important factor for Senior Vice President Hope. Prior strategic plans had less consideration for the financial components of what was being proposed, but in the revised process the senior vice president or one of his staff is engaged in every planning meeting and is providing essential financial modeling and advice.

Ongoing Work and Future Plan Developments

As the strategic plan was in development, Colgate also introduced several new initiatives, including new campus academic initiatives, capital projects, and financial aid commitments. These initiatives will be part of the new strategic plan or will provide a base for expanded efforts within the broader plan.

Supporting the Life of the Faculty

One element of the new strategic plan involves greater support for faculty. In an interview, Senior Vice President Hope observed that finding ways to potentially decrease course loads and ensure more time for scholarship may receive focus in the new plan (personal interview, March 11, 2019). Such a provision would certainly echo elements found in President Casey's vision statement, where he noted Colgate's historic commitment to the development and maintenance of "a research-intensive faculty."

New Interdisciplinary Initiatives

Another element of academic initiatives in the upcoming plan includes support for new interdisciplinary curricular interests. These initiatives, one in the sciences and one in the arts, are meant to bridge different departments and encourage collaboration. The commitment to the sciences initiative was announced in 2019, when President Casey shared with the Colgate community the creation of a new Mind, Brain, and Behavior Initiative (MBB) through a $15 million donation from Trustee Emeritus Robert Hung Ngai Ho '56, (Schnell, 2019). The creation of MBB through the Ho donation will simultaneously support the broader interdisciplinary initiative and the renovation and expansion of research and building space on campus.

In addition to MBB, both President Casey and Senior Vice President Hope noted the likely development of an initiative in the arts (B. Casey, personal interview, March 1, 2019). President Casey indicated that, while the initiative is yet to have a formal name, it will involve the arts, innovation, design, and entrepreneurship. If the new strategic plan maintains this focus, President Casey is prepared to commit a large portion of the debt acquired in 2017 to launch the effort (J. Hope, personal interview, March 11, 2019).

These two initiatives will not radically change the curriculum or shift Colgate away from the liberal arts. As President Casey noted in an interview, these changes are adaptive rather than revolutionary (personal interview, March 1, 2019). There will be new course development and new faculty hires relative to these initiatives, but the core elements of the institution will remain the same.

Elevating Career Services

Colgate also opened a new building for career services in 2019, a project that was featured in a *New York Times* article, "More Colleges Are Playing the Long Game" (Hannon, 2018). President Casey noted that, while career services and attention on outcomes for students have been a strength for Colgate, the institution made a symbolic statement by constructing a new career services building on the main quad of campus (personal interview, March 1, 2019). It is now included in the campus admissions tour, the university provides an additional special information session for prospective students related to career services, and Colgate is generating new career services publications for students and families. Initial reactions from visiting students and families have been quite positive and differentiate Colgate from its peers.

New Residence Halls and Ongoing Commitments to Residential Life

Colgate's other recent capital project is the construction of 2 new residence halls designed to house 200 students. The construction of these buildings represents the institution's commitment to the living and learning spaces that are central to the Colgate experience. The prior strategic plan emphasized that the ultimate goal for residential life at the university is to have all first-year students engaged in a residential learning community (Colgate University, 2014).

The new dorms will allow the university to take less desirable housing out of use and provide flexibility for the university to consider limited enrollment growth. As an institution that prides itself on its residential life—it is one of the four key elements of Colgate, as noted by President Casey

(2018)—it would be unsurprising if the new plan outlined a large commitment to residential life.

Colgate's Financial Aid Policy

One component of the prior strategic plan was consideration of a need-blind admission policy. While the ambitious goal of operating need blind is still in the minds of Colgate leadership, it will likely remain aspirational until the university can acquire significant funding toward, and growth of, the endowment to support such an undertaking. Colgate already pledges to meet 100% of a student's demonstrated need. In conversation with President Casey and Senior Vice President Hope, both were excited about the prospect of taking the next significant step toward supporting students in affording a Colgate education—adopting a no-loan financial aid policy (B. Casey, personal interview, March 1, 2019). This commitment will almost certainly be a part of the new plan. Providing no-loan financial aid aligns directly with President Casey's fundamental goal for the future of "attracting outstanding students" outlined in his vision statement and is a concrete commitment to attracting and enrolling outstanding students in an increasingly financially strapped marketplace.

Figure 4.2. Colgate University at a glance.

Endowment	$920 million
Student to Faculty Ratio	9:1
Enrollment	2,894
Four-Year Graduation Rate	88%
Six-Year Graduation Rate	91%
Key Elements of the Curriculum	56 majors Classic liberal arts curriculum Core curriculum has not changed since 1920s and remains an essential part of the Colgate experience

Colgate University, n.d.a, n.d.c; U.S. Department of Education, 2019b.

Conclusion

Colgate University's historic strength as a liberal arts institution is serving the university well in the increasingly uncertain world of higher education. Rather than making major changes, Colgate, as President Casey observed, is doubling down on what it does well and is approaching change adaptively; this allows the institution to meet shifting expectations of its current and prospective students and families while retaining the key elements that form the bedrock of the university's identity.

President Casey's vision statement thoughtfully reflects on the prior 200 years of Colgate's history, interwoven with the strength of the most recent strategic plan, and provides clarity and direction for the next strategic plan and Colgate's third century. While radical changes may not be taking place, strategic initiatives and developments in career planning, residential life, financial aid, and the curricular interests of brain sciences and arts and entrepreneurship provide the essential momentum and incremental change needed for both maintaining the strength of the institution and the charting of a promising future in the midst of dramatic changes across the larger higher education landscape.

Notes

1 The Commons program facilitates a group living, advising, dining, academic, and service experience for students (Colgate University, n.d.d).
2 In 2017, Colgate, leveraging a favorable market for taking on debt given low rates and advantageous terms, took on $100 million in debt for future use.

5

UNDERSTANDING THE
INTEGRATED MODEL

The integrated model for small colleges and universities is so named because the institutions that fit this model attempt to integrate the liberal arts and professional programs. Many also integrate their bachelor's and master's degree offerings, with targeted graduate programs that build from their undergraduate strengths, often in a 4 + 1 program structure.

The integrated model captures many of the institutions that began as small liberal arts colleges and, by adding professional and graduate programs, became comprehensive universities. Their identity and place in American higher education has been the subject of significant discussion. In the early and mid-1990s, there was a great deal of ferment concerning the classification of colleges and universities, and in 1994, the Carnegie Foundation for the Advancement of Teaching revised its well-known higher education classification system, creating a master's (comprehensive) category for institutions that awarded both bachelor's and master's degrees. This revised classification included many small colleges and universities that integrated the liberal arts and the professions (Evangelauf, 1994).

The new category was not clear in its description and indeed seemed to be composed largely of institutions that did not fit neatly into either the liberal arts category or the research category. In the midst of these shifts, a thoughtful conversation developed about independent small and midsize institutions that fit a more integrated model; they had both liberal arts programs and professional offerings that were designed to reinforce each other. These institutions were often lost in the shadow of their wealthier traditional liberal arts colleagues or had less visible presence, with fewer obvious champions, than their public university peers. But many had quietly added programs that served their region, such as business or education, and most retained a strong commitment to the essence of the liberal arts. These colleges and universities were aptly describe, in a well-circulated essay by the then-provost at Redlands University, Frank Wong, as the "Ugly Ducklings" of higher education (Wong, 1990). His argument was that smaller campuses that integrated the liberal arts and professional education were poorly understood and equally undervalued. His thoughtful essay gave rise to a larger movement toward developing the unique characteristics of these institutions, with a focus on the value of blending the strengths of liberal arts education with the practical aspects of professional and graduate education.

Within this context, a group of private colleges and universities began discussing how they could create a more purposeful, integrated approach to teaching and learning. While they had begun to offer a range of programs in the liberal arts and the professions, there was little cohesion or understanding of their work. They had expanded their programs, but they lacked a clear identity.

The notion of an intentional and productive integration to define campuses that fit the integrated model grew from this ongoing conversation, including important intellectual contributions from notable higher education leaders such as Ernest Boyer, Alexander Astin, and Eugene Rice. The effective comprehensive campus was envisioned as a purposeful hybrid of the liberal arts and research institutions. A new organization, the New American Colleges and Universities (NAC&U), was formed to curate best practices and offer professional development opportunities for faculty, staff, and leadership at the strongest of these institutions. Today, NAC&U defines itself as "a national consortium of selective small-to-mid-size independent colleges and universities dedicated to the purposeful integration of liberal education, professional studies, and civic engagement" (NAC&U, n.d.)

Membership in the NAC&U consortium is a relatively modest 24 campuses. But their focused commitment to understanding and defining the most effective educational approaches for the integrated model makes the organization a useful benchmark in understanding the essential aspects of these institutions. The integrated model includes a larger category of institutions that offer both liberal arts and professional programs and that seek to purposefully integrate the two. The accompanying campus profiles will feature one institution that is a member of NAC&U and one that is not a member to help illustrate the range of possibilities within the integrated model.

Defining Features of the Integrated Model

Institutions in the integrated model are defined by their programmatic offerings in the liberal arts and the professions, by their programs at both the undergraduate and graduate level, and by their commitment to primarily campus-based education. Institutions in this model have retained a set of core liberal arts programs that infuse the undergraduate experience regardless of the major a student chooses. But in addition, these campuses also offer preprofessional and professional degrees. For example, they will offer bachelor of arts degrees in traditional disciplines such as English or history, while also offering degrees in professional or preprofessional areas such as nursing, entrepreneurship, or the health sciences.

The integrated model campuses also offer targeted graduate degree programs. Some of these graduate degrees are in the traditional liberal arts disciplines and focus on moving students toward academic careers including teaching and research. Frequently, graduate programs at these institutions are also offered in professional areas such as law, education, business, or the health sciences—degrees that align explicitly with a career rather than focusing solely on the educational journey. At both the graduate and undergraduate level, integrated model campuses are committed to drawing strength from the best of liberal arts colleges—particularly including a residential community with a core education focused on close reading, analysis, and communication—and the best of research institutions—including focused research and applied learning.

Within this diversity of offerings, the integrated model campus retains a commitment to a liberal arts general education for undergraduates. The general education model is designed to infuse the liberal arts into all educational work, as well as serve as an introduction for students who go on to receive a degree in a traditional liberal arts discipline.

For most institutions in the integrated model, a large percentage of students reside on or near campus; it is primarily a campus-based learning approach, not a commuter model. They may offer some online or hybrid courses, and they may deliver some targeted programs beyond the main campus. But the majority of courses are provided on their home campus, in a regular classroom, with a standard credit hours format.

Because of this commitment to place-based learning, many campuses in the integrated model have developed programs and activities that are specifically designed to serve their region. This may include an active service-learning or civic engagement program that is connected to the region. For example, Wagner College, located on Staten Island, New York, includes a robust service-learning program that works with Port Richmond, a nearby community with a large immigrant population (Wagner College, 2019).

Connection to place may also be illustrated through research or degree programs that serve site-specific industries, such as museum studies, hospitality, or healthy aging. For example, Linfield College is located near the

Oregon wine country and offers a major in wine studies as well as a Center for Wine Education (Linfield College, 2019). Programs are developed based on regional and civic concerns, and—as we will see in the profiles of two of these institutions—with a clear recognition of the demographics of the communities and prospective degree-seeking students in the region.

Finally, because of their campus-based delivery, residential nature, and traditional program structure, campuses in the integrated model tend to recruit, and to largely be populated with, undergraduate students who are in the traditional age range for college students of 18 to 26. These institutions recruit their entering undergraduate class at the usual college fairs, working with college counselors and high schools, and through outreach to parents as well as prospective students.

Inherent Strengths of the Integrated Model

The integrated model, broadly understood, is the most common presentation of small independent colleges and universities today. As we have seen, there are significant challenges—primarily in the form of student recruitment and financial stability—associated with operating a campus with a purely liberal arts focus. The integrated model is the most common response to this challenge, adding and integrating new programs alongside the liberal arts and bringing the whole into a coherent presentation of the campus.

When thoughtfully developed, the effective integration of the liberal arts and the professions can be one of the great educational strengths of the integrated model. It ensures that students with professional degrees also acquire skills usually associated with the liberal arts such as critical thinking, effective communication, close analysis, and creative problem-solving. Further, this integration proposes that students earning degrees in the liberal arts will have the opportunity to engage in the practical application that helps their education correlate to life beyond the academy.

A potential fiscal strength of the integrated model—indeed, the primary reason many of these institutions adopted the model—is that by providing preprofessional and professional programs alongside their traditional liberal arts offerings, they increase their attractiveness to a broader range of students. Adding targeted graduate programs further extends the number and type of students the campus can serve. Like diversifying a financial portfolio, this approach offers some ballast against the ebbs and flows in demand for particular majors and programs.

Diversity of programs can also expand an institution's network of alumni and friends. Developing programs that respond to the needs of local businesses can help ensure a postgraduation path for students and provides local expertise from which to build a program. Pursuing research and establishing civic engagement activities that respond to regional issues ties the institution to its area in ways that help build fiscal and social capital. By coupling its programs with regional issues and markets, a campus can strengthen its own position while serving as an anchor for the area.

Inherent Challenges of the Integrated Model

However, many of the integrated model's challenges correlate directly to the aforementioned potential strengths. So many small colleges and universities have now added graduate and professional programs that their existence now offers little market distinction. Indeed, it can sometimes be difficult to differentiate an independent institution in the integrated model from a public comprehensive university, much less from its regional private competitors. This lack of differentiation can make campuses vulnerable, especially when state or federal governments implement public policy that elevates the attractiveness of regional public institutions. For example, a free four-year public college initiative was introduced in the state of New York especially in the first year of its availability, the visibility and financial incentives of that program put tremendous pressure on independent New York colleges and universities in the integrated model. And while differentiation alone may not inure a campus to the concerns such policies present, the lack of clear distinction in academic program offerings between regional publics and the many private institutions that are offering similar programs can be a significant challenge.

It can also be difficult for an institution in the integrated model to maintain the desired program mix. Some campuses that have health sciences or business programs, for example, find that their clearest route to stabilize enrollment is to expand those programs. In the process, they often also shift the balance of academic offerings from the core liberal arts to professional and graduate programs. This shift in program enrollment and resource distribution can raise several significant issues. Such changes put pressure on the alignment of faculty to program; if long-tenured faculty are in low-demand programs and untenured or newly tenured faculty are in the high-demand programs, it is more likely that a schism, rather than integration, will be the result.

Further, if the programs with high market demand are also programs that require substantial staff support or specialized equipment—for example, practicum placements, simulation labs, or independent accreditation— they also need additional staff, faculty, and infrastructure. In the short run,

developing or expanding programs requires planning and up-front investment. Over time, such shifts in focus can undermine institutional identity
and mission as campus investment moves away from the liberal arts and
toward the professional programs.

Contemporary Examples of the Integrated Model

The addition of professional programs to the liberal arts core in the integrated
model is usually informed by institutional history and regional distinctions,
as well as the campus's need to diversify programs to remain competitive.
The ways in which they develop and continue to evolve are well illustrated in
the accompanying profiles of Trinity Washington University and California
Lutheran University. Located on different coasts with equally different institutional histories, these two campuses provide instructive illustrations of how
an independent institution can employ the integrated model to aid fiscal
stability and advance mission.

Trinity Washington University began as a women's Catholic liberal
arts college in the late 1800s. Today, it remains an undergraduate women's
college (graduate programs are coed). Trinity maintained its singular commitment to the liberal arts for nearly a century, but by the 1980s, the college was experiencing enrollment and fiscal challenges that amounted to an
existential crisis. Its ongoing approach of offering only a Catholic liberal
education to primarily middle-class White women was no longer drawing students to the campus. The challenge was highlighted by the college's
location in urban Washington DC, where the institution was surrounded
by a highly diverse population that the campus did not serve. The transformation of Trinity from a fairly insular undergraduate liberal arts women's
college in the traditional model to a diverse and dynamic university in the
integrated model was a multidecade process—a process that ultimately
saved the institution.

In contrast to Trinity, California Lutheran University's (Cal Lutheran's)
path to becoming an institution in the integrated model involved a less defin-
itive break from its history. Founded in the 1950s, Cal Lutheran began with
programs in the liberal arts and religion. As the college grew to a university,
it also expanded to professional programs and added graduate degrees to its
offerings. Today, Cal Lutheran has a School of Arts and Sciences in the traditional mold but also houses a Graduate School of Education, a Graduate
School of Psychology, a School of Management, and a theological seminary.
While it has five off-site locations, they are modest in size and focused on
specific programs; the theological seminary, for example, is located several

hundred miles north of the main campus. Its main campus is the hub of educational programming, and over half of its undergraduate students reside on campus.

The ways in which Trinity and Cal Lutheran became campuses in the integrated model are illustrated in more detail in the accompanying profiles. They are very different institutions. But it is instructive to consider, despite their differences, the commonalities in the ways they are adapting to the challenges facing small colleges. Most notable is their proactive embrace of the diverse populations in their region. More than expanded student recruitment, both Trinity and Cal Lutheran adopted a number of programs and policies designed to not only reach a more diverse student population but also ensure the success of those students.

Both campuses also focused on the needs of their community. They built programs in areas that aligned with the business and civic demands of the region and continue to evaluate their success at least partially on the strength of their regional ties.

And both campuses retain a strong commitment to liberal education. At their core they offer both robust general education requirements and disciplinary majors and minors in the traditional liberal arts disciplines, even as they have added graduate and professional programs.

PROFILE OF AN INTEGRATED MODEL INSTITUTION: CALIFORNIA LUTHERAN UNIVERSITY

A portion of this profile was developed by Madeline Rachel Mortimore while an EdM student at the Harvard Graduate School of Education.

Cal Lutheran is nestled in the idyllic town of Thousand Oaks, California, located between Santa Barbara and Los Angeles. Founded in 1959 as the first Lutheran college in the southwest, California Lutheran College was accredited in 1962 as a liberal arts college by the Western Association of Schools and Colleges (WASC) and graduated its first class in 1964. Relatively young by the standards of many independent colleges and universities, Cal Lutheran has seen remarkable growth and evolution in the decades since its inception.

Founded with the support of 5 national Lutheran churches and established with the gift of a 130-acre parcel of land, Cal Lutheran's mission was to help students grow as individuals in order to contribute in the best possible way to the world. The college grew through the 1960s but also faced serious financial challenges, and by 1970 the young college was facing bankruptcy.

The college survived through the introduction of new programs, increased visibility through athletic success (particularly in football), and assistance in retiring some of the college's debt. At the same time, the college added graduate degrees and teacher credentialing to its academic offerings, expanding its traditional liberal arts curriculum to reach a broader range of students. As a result of these actions Cal Lutheran weathered the crisis because of a reduced debt load and student enrollment growth; by the early 1970s the student population expanded to nearly 1,000. These actions also foreshadowed an institution that was willing—indeed, often found it necessary—to respond nimbly to internal and external challenges.

As might be expected of the first Lutheran institution established in the southwest, during the founding era of Cal Lutheran, its religious identity was central to the student experience, and 78% of the student body identified as Lutheran. This, too, changed over time. Beginning in the early 1980s, the college actively began recruiting international students and students of all ages, and various cultural, religious, and ethnic backgrounds, and the student population became more diverse. By the mid-1990s, approximately 25% of the student body identified as Lutheran, and a small but ongoing population of international students began to develop. Today 4% of undergraduate students and 21% of graduate students are international. As we will see in the recent initiatives undertaken by Cal Lutheran, this diversification, too, would presage an equally intentional, but more profound, shift in diversifying the student body.

Along with the shift in student profile, academic program offerings continued to expand to respond to emerging demand. In the late 1980s and early 1990s, new off-campus centers were opened to reach targeted student populations and serve the region. In addition, Cal Lutheran was particularly prescient in adding programs in several important areas at a relatively early date, including a new major in computer science in 1983 and an online master's in business administration in 2005.

Today, Cal Lutheran's mission is to "educate leaders for a global society who are strong in character and judgment, confident in their identity and vocation, and committed to service and justice" (California Lutheran University, n.d.a). Its current undergraduate enrollment stands at just over 3,000, and the total student population has steadily increased over the past decade, with enrollment as of fall 2018 at an all-time high of 4,400.

Cal Lutheran offers undergraduate programs in 38 majors and 40 minors, with the option to enroll in a 4 + 1 program, where students can complete an undergraduate and master's degree in 5 years. The most popular undergraduate degrees are business administration, criminal justice, and psychology. The majority of students are enrolled in the College of Arts and Sciences. At the graduate level, Cal Lutheran offers both master's and doctoral degrees, with an emphasis on educational leadership, psychology, theology, and business.

A Model of the New American College and University

Cal Lutheran is a member of the NAC&U consortium and embodies that organization's commitment to the "purposeful integration of liberal education, professional studies, and civic engagement" (NAC&U, n.d.). Both the ways in which the university integrates the liberal arts and professional programs and its commitment to civic engagement and service are worth noting.

Because Cal Lutheran adopted some targeted professional programs relatively early in its history—it was well known for its education program by the 1970s—the integration of the liberal arts and professional programs has been both natural and intentional. As President Chris Kimball noted, "the culture and the structure have allowed a broader base of cooperation and collegiality . . . faculty don't see themselves as one versus the other. The professional programs have been there all along and are seen as a core piece rather than an add-on" (personal interview, April 15, 2019). This culture is informal but reinforced by the organization of Cal Lutheran's academic programs. For example, an emerging program in data science shares faculty with existing programs in mathematics and in management. Similarly, an emerging program in music industry will have faculty from both the music department and School of Management.

Along with a high degree of interdisciplinarity, Cal Lutheran embeds service and civic engagement into the student experience from the time a student enrolls. As part of their initial orientation, all first-year students are involved in a day-long service project coordinated with the nearby City of Ventura. By front-loading this experience, the university aims to establish an expectation of service and of civic engagement. All clubs and organizations, along with athletics, have a service component, and the guidelines—such as requiring that 80% of athletes from a given team participate together—build a sense of community and an expectation of service as a core value for the institution. This identification underscores the university's commitment to retaining its roots in a religious education dedicated to helping students discover their purpose, while offering both the liberal arts and professional programs.

Responding to New Realities and New Demographics

President Chris Kimball began his tenure in 2008, having served as provost and vice president for academic affairs at Cal Lutheran prior to moving into the presidency. President Kimball knew his institution well and had helped grow and diversify the academic program offerings. He was also aware of the changing demographics of the prospective student population, particularly in the Southern California area where Cal Lutheran is located, and where it recruits a majority of its students. President Kimball launched three strategic initiatives specifically designed to respond to emerging student demographics.

Led by Vice President of Enrollment and Marketing Matthew Ward, the first major initiative was to intentionally establish Cal Lutheran as a Hispanic-serving institution (HSI). This process took approximately eight years and included a focused outreach strategy in admissions, as well as an evaluation of and adjustment to institutional support systems. HSI designation was achieved in 2016, when Cal Lutheran met the standard of a student body that is at least 25% Hispanic for a series of years.

The university was committed to not only providing access to a more diverse student body but also serving those students well and incorporating inclusivity on campus. The vision, as articulated by President Kimball, was not only for Cal Lutheran to be a Hispanic *enrolling* institution by achieving diversity in numbers, but to become a truly Hispanic-*serving* institution.

Both the process and the outcomes of becoming an HSI have been impressive at Cal Lutheran. As the campus sought to achieve HSI status, President Kimball created a task force of administration and faculty that developed the entire strategy, from admission and retention to curriculum development and implementation. After achieving HSI designation, the task force expanded, adding to its membership new hires that were the result of grant funding from the HSI designation.

In addition to the task force, Cal Lutheran used two external groups to assist with the admissions and retention process, as well as groups to help establish inclusivity on campus as the university moved toward HSI status. An initiative to increase the number of Latinx staff and faculty was launched shortly after achieving HSI designation, with the goal of creating a professional population that was more representative of the student body.

The establishment of Cal Lutheran as an HSI institution helped the campus secure several important major grants from the federal government.

One grant, called the ALLIES in STEM initiative, provided funds for a dramatic effort to increase student success. It included support for four new staff positions and a partial faculty position, provided funds for professional development, and supported training in cultural competency. It also supported the creation of a new ALLIES center, a physical space to house the program.

This initial grant funding was crucial to launching a series of activities designed to improve student success. Among those activities were a STEM Academy, a Summer Bridge program, focused instruction and tutoring, and outreach to regional schools and community colleges with a large Hispanic population.

The results of these efforts have been gratifying. Along with improved academic performance, the campus has seen increased retention in STEM majors and more underrepresented students graduating with STEM degrees (California Lutheran University, n.d.b). Beyond retention and graduation rates, the university assesses inclusivity through both student and staff climate surveys.

As a result of the HSI designation, there have also been additions to Cal Lutheran's degree programs. New bilingual programs have been added, and new satellite campus locations have been established that are situated closer to communities with a large Hispanic population. At the graduate level, there are several programs that are directed toward Spanish-speaking and bilingual schools.

A second major initiative has built on the campus's historic commitment to inclusion in another way: an expansive interfaith initiative. Led by interfaith strategist Rahuldeep Gill, Cal Lutheran has developed a series of programs that intentionally bring groups from different faiths together to increase understanding, explore cultures, and take action. More than simply conversing, these groups identify common values and work together to address issues. As President Kimball stated, the goal is to "move beyond awareness, beyond acceptance, to action—to answer the question: 'What can we do together?'" (personal interview, April 15, 2019). For example, the groups have explored what each faith tradition teaches about responding to those who are suffering in the local community. After discussing the issue from a multitude of faith perspectives—Protestant, Catholic, Jewish, Muslim, secular—the groups recognized that each faith, in its own way, asked its adherents to respond with compassion to the suffering of others. Instead of simply acknowledging this link the groups have identified projects to undertake together. One such project involved Muslim and Jewish students creating medical kits for Syrian refugees.

This interfaith work has become integral to the campus culture and to the student experience. Along with projects and activities, the students socialize, talk, and work across faiths. Passover Seder may be organized by the Jewish students, but fully half of those attending are likely to be Muslim. Similarly, becoming an HSI was not an isolated effort but designed to expand the university's inclusivity in a broader manner. Thus, it was discussed with the existing student groups to generate ideas for the entire campus to use HSI designation to create a more diverse and more inclusive institution.

The third major initiative to respond to a changing student profile has focused on reducing the cost of attendance for students. Recognizing the anxiety about the cost of college and understanding the changing socioeconomic reality of the traditional college-age population, Cal Lutheran established two programs designed to address financial concerns and increase enrollment. The first is known as the Public Price Promise. Like most private colleges in the west, Cal Lutheran has admissions cross-applications with many of the public universities in the state. The Public Price Promise was created to address cost concerns and to highlight Cal Lutheran as a financially viable, educationally competitive alternative to these public campuses. It is a scholarship program designed for California students who have been admitted to the most selective public institutions in the state. If a student is admitted to any of the six most selective University of California campuses, they immediately qualify for Cal Lutheran's Public Price Promise scholarship. The scholarship covers the difference in average cost of attendance between Cal Lutheran and the public university and aligns with the university's usual merit aid programs. The assumption is that if the anxiety about price is addressed, students and families will realize they will get an equally strong, if not better, education at Cal Lutheran.

An additional program designed to address the cost of college is the 4 to Finish program. Recognizing that it can be difficult for students to gain access to classes and programs at the large and crowded state institutions, this program highlights the personalization and access of Cal Lutheran. The 4 to Finish program promises that any student who commits to regular academic advising sessions is guaranteed to graduate within four years. If they do not, Cal Lutheran will cover the remainder of their tuition and other attendance expenses.

Both financial strategies were developed after analyzing data such as degree attainment and financial aid per student. Both have proven to be attractive to students who might otherwise not have considered Cal Lutheran.

Outcomes

In order to increase financial stability, respond to changes in demographics, and embrace its mission, California Lutheran has focused on both enrollment growth and thoughtful diversification of its student body. Total enrollment has increased by nearly 1,000 students in the last decade, and the current enrollment of more than 4,400 is the largest in the university's history. The student body is diverse and reflects the region in which the university resides: 32% identify as Hispanic, 6% identify as 2 or more races, 5% identify as Asian, 3% identify as Black, and 8% are international. Approximately 20% of students are classified as first-generation students, as a result of proactive efforts to recruit and admit more students from this underrepresented group.

It is particularly impressive that as Cal Lutheran has grown and diversified its student body, measures of student success have also increased. The 4-year graduation rate is 69%, up from 50% in 2005, and the 6-year graduation rate is 71%, up from 66% in 2008. The first-year retention rate is 85%. These measures suggest that the intentionality and care given to becoming an HSI, to supporting first-generation students, and to promoting active interfaith work are serving the expanded student body well.

Figure 5.1. California Lutheran University at a glance.

Endowment	$108.8 million
Student:Faculty Ratio	16:1
Enrollment	4,236
Four-Year Graduation Rate	69%
Six-Year Graduation Rate	71%
Key Elements of the Curriculum	37 majors "Core 21" general education curriculum Preprofessional advising tracks for engineering, law, and medicine 4 + 1 master's degree program

California Lutheran University, 2018; U.S. Department of Education, 2019a.

PROFILE OF AN INTEGRATED MODEL INSTITUTON: TRINITY WASHINGTON UNIVERSITY

Field research and draft compilation of this campus profile conducted by Hillary Casavant while an Ed.M. student at the Harvard Graduate School of Education

A Brief History

Trinity Washington University, located in urban Washington DC, was founded in 1897 as the first U.S. university to provide women access to a Catholic liberal arts education. Courses were primarily taught by the Sisters of Notre Dame de Namur, who kept institutional costs low by working without pay through contributed service. In the 1960s, Trinity enrolled 1,000 undergraduate women. But when DC area universities like Georgetown and Catholic University became coeducational, enrollment at Trinity began to plummet. Following the retirement of its longtime president in 1975, Trinity struggled to stop the downward enrollment trend. But change would not come until Pat McGuire, a Trinity alumna with a career in law and higher education fundraising, came to the helm in 1989. Her long tenure has led the intentional transformation of Trinity from a traditional liberal arts school into a university in the integrated model.

Mission

Trinity's mission, adopted in 2000, has four pillars:

1. Commitment to the education of women through the undergraduate women's college and by advancing principles of equity, justice, and honor in the education of women and men in all other programs;
2. Foundation for learning in the liberal arts through curriculum design and emphasis on the knowledge, skills, and values of liberal learning;
3. Integration for learning with professional preparation through applied and experiential learning opportunities in all programs;
4. Grounding in the mission of the Sisters of Notre Dame de Namur and the Catholic tradition, welcoming persons of all faiths in the promotion of social justice. (Trinity, n.d.c.)

Enrollment, Student Profile, and Major Programs

When President Pat McGuire assumed the role in 1989, Trinity offered 50 different major programs but employed just 40 full-time faculty members and enrolled a scant 300 undergraduate students, who were largely White, middle-class, Catholic women of traditional college age. Today, the school enrolls 1,100 undergraduates—predominantly African American and Latina women from the DC area—in its College of Arts and Sciences and School of Nursing and Health Professions. Approximately 80% of the school's students receive Pell grants, and 10% of undergraduates are undocumented (P. McGuire, personal interview, November 19, 2018). Trinity offers bachelor's and associate's degrees in 12 disciplines, with the most popular programs in nursing, biology and biochemistry, health services, counseling, business, criminal justice, psychology, communication, and education (U.S. Department of Education, 2019c). The graduate programs enroll a total of 700 students in the School of Education, School of Business and Graduate Studies, and the School of Professional Studies.

Trinity: A University in the Integrated Model

Throughout the 1990s, Trinity underwent dramatic and sometimes controversial changes—what its administrators refer to as a "paradigm shift" (P. McGuire, personal interview, November 19, 2018). They established a strategic vision for long-term sustainability, informed by the core elements of Trinity's mission as well as an assessment of emerging student demographics. They identified their strongest academic programs and seized new opportunities that aligned with the school's strengths and liberal arts mission. Following the tenets of the NAC&U, Trinity sustained its emphasis on civic responsibility while strengthening enrollment by adding professional programs that met local market demands in areas such as healthcare and education. Through this model, Trinity remains committed to ensuring that its professional degree students also gain core skills associated with the liberal arts.

A Series of Innovations

The transformation began once Trinity identified its strengths and weaknesses. While the undergraduate school was floundering in the early 1990s, Trinity's weekend college, which provided adult education to predominantly Black women, had nearly double the enrollment of the traditional core. The School of Education was also well enrolled. Evaluating this reality and seeing the new student demographic trends, McGuire believed Trinity could not cling to a rigid notion of what a small private college should be. Instead, it needed to reinvent itself and diversify its approach—financially, programmatically, and demographically—in order to survive. Administrators also initially questioned whether Trinity should remain an all-women's college. But when they evaluated peer institutions, they found that most other women's colleges that had opened the school to men saw only minimal enrollment gains. The cost of Title IX compliance and facility updates would also have put a considerable strain on Trinity's limited budget. In addition, although DC was replete with coed liberal arts universities, Trinity was the sole provider in the niche women's college market. So it embraced its identity as a women's college and committed to serving the needs of low-income, minority students in the city. At the time a provocative decision, it was in fact a return to Trinity's roots: Once again, Trinity would provide a liberal arts education to women who could not previously access it (P. McGuire, personal interview, November 19, 2018).

In conjunction with this transformation in the student body, the school recognized that it could not sustain itself solely on its undergraduate education. Throughout the 1990s, Trinity opened new graduate programs to attract a different population and meet the needs of a new generation of students. After analyzing programs at other schools and weighing risks and benefits, Trinity expanded the offerings of its coed School of Professional Studies and developed more career-oriented majors in areas such as communication, business, and criminal justice to match the interests of its new target demographics. In 2006, Trinity's School of Professional Studies also partnered with other community organizations to open an associate's degree–granting adult program in a low-income neighborhood, a decision that has reinforced Trinity's relationship with DC legislators (P. McGuire, personal interview, December 17, 2018).

In 2006, another major shift in academic programs took place when Trinity began to offer nursing and other healthcare undergraduate programs (Trinity Washington University, 2014). Although it had provided pre-med education in the past, Trinity saw a need from local industries as well as interest from their target student population to develop more programs in the healthcare field. Most recently, Trinity has established an associate's program for early childhood education to meet new DC requirements.

Within these curricular changes, liberal arts remained at the core of the institution. While providing practical career preparation through hands-on experience, research opportunities, and required internships, Trinity instills the holistic tenets of a liberal arts education, giving students the skills to think critically, solve problems, examine their values and belief systems, and embrace diversity (C. Ocampo, personal interview, December 17, 2018).

The Change Process

The innovations that Trinity adopted emerged from a robust strategic plan that has continued to evolve over the last 30 years. The plan is based on data from exemplary peer institutions and their models for student retention and degree completion. The administration decided early on that it would not work with external advisors or consultants in order to design the change. Limited by a tight budget and virtually no investment capital, Trinity instead took advantage of conferences through the Association of American Colleges and Universities (AAC&U), as well as Middle States accreditation resources, to learn best practices and gain feedback from peer colleges. New programs in nursing and other fields were supported through budget reallocation. Each new investment that Trinity chose to make was closely aligned with the strategic plan and mission and focused on enrollment and retention. Throughout the process, it leveraged the talents and resources already in place (K. Gerlach, personal interview, December 17, 2019). In order to implement transformative change, administrators worked both within and around shared governance. Early in McGuire's presidency, Trinity conducted a careful program review to evaluate which academic majors could be fiscally sustainable in the future. These hard economic data was shared with faculty members, and a team of senior faculty were given the charge to determine which 16 of the 50 majors Trinity could afford to sustain. Despite initial resistance and understandable turmoil, faculty ultimately voted to reduce majors in order to keep Trinity's doors open.

As Trinity began to enroll a new demographic of students, faculty also expressed concern that the student population was unprepared for higher education. But administrators worked tirelessly to shift perspectives. McGuire would repeatedly remind faculty that "it's not the students who are unprepared—it's we who are unprepared for them" (personal interview, November 19, 2018). Trinity needed to identify new ways to foster student success with this new population. At Trinity, access and excellence would not be mutually exclusive (C. Ocampo, personal interview, December 17, 2018).

While maintaining and arguably improving the quality of education, Trinity underwent significant curriculum revisions in order to better meet the needs of its students. Shifting away from the open course selection process of traditional liberal arts colleges, Trinity adopted a scaffolded course sequence, broken down into applied meta-major pathways that students can follow to obtain their degree. For a time, Trinity provided noncredit remedial courses for academically underprepared students but soon discovered that these courses hampered success. It shifted to its current corequisite model, embedding additional learning supports into college-level classes. First-year success rates improved dramatically once Trinity adopted this model. Trinity also hired instructional specialists in math, critical reading, and collegiate writing to support student learning as well as faculty development in teaching these subjects. Trinity reacted nimbly throughout the academic change process. Its small size allows it to respond quickly to failing initiatives and build energy around new solutions (D. Van Camp, personal interview, December 17, 2018). Its size also makes administrators more accessible to students, which in turn allows administrators to identify problems more easily (P. Lewis, personal interview, December 17, 2018).

Trinity also underwent significant changes in pedagogy, shifting from the traditional lecture-based model to inclusive excellence pedagogy and multivariate teaching styles that foster active learning. The curricular and pedagogical shifts were gradually adopted by faculty who recognized these changes were essential for student success and Trinity's survival. This was a long-term transformation, and many faculty members who initially resisted the changes adapted to the new approach or retired, allowing Trinity to hire new teaching staff who supported the vision of a diverse student body and an integrated structure that embraced both the liberal arts and professional programs. Trinity also developed a new system of promotion and tenure that evaluates faculty based on their ability to support and embrace the current student population. The hiring of new faculty from underrepresented backgrounds has subsequently opened connections with other opportunities and networks; for example, the recent hiring of young women of color to the science faculty brought new professional ties to organizations that promote undergraduate research for minority students (P. McGuire, personal interview, November 19, 2018).

Throughout its innovations over the last three decades, Trinity has walked the delicate line between tradition and change. And as might be expected, administrators faced immense resistance and controversy as Trinity began to implement the more radical changes. Prominent alumnae resisted the demographic shift in Trinity's student body and feared the school was lowering its academic standards for these populations. But over time, new leadership in the alumnae association—leaders who embraced the newly diverse student population and curricular changes—began to serve as ambassadors and rallied their classmates behind Trinity's mission (P. McGuire, personal interview, November 19, 2018).

President McGuire believes the support of her board of trustees in the face of faculty and alumnae resistance was essential in making Trinity's changes possible. But she emphasizes that the change process can never be complete. "Accepting change is a constant part of life in higher ed," she says. "It's essential to keep moving ahead" (P. McGuire personal interview, November 19, 2018).

Outcomes

Trinity achieved a key milestone in its change process in 2000, when both enrollment and finances stabilized. Around this time, the school held a centennial celebration; launched a capital campaign; and secured sufficient philanthropic support to open a sports center, the first new building on campus in 40 years. This era served as a rallying point for the community and propelled the campus toward its second milestone, an exceptional Middle States review in 2006. With no requirements for follow-up reporting, it was the first clean report Trinity had received in decades. The subsequent success of the new nursing program boosted enrollment and generated a financial surplus, which was put toward building a new academic center that opened in 2016 with state-of-the-art science and nursing labs. As it looks forward to 2025, Trinity's latest strategic plan includes an enrollment goal of 2,800 students; fundraising goals to increase the annual fund to $1.5 million and additional fundraising for special projects to a minimum of $3 million; and new program development to improve retention and completion, while maintaining a values-centered education and a high level of academic rigor (Trinity Washington University, n.d.d).

Markers for Success

Early in its transformation, Trinity identified a group of 25 benchmark institutions with similar student bodies, structures, and resources. It uses these benchmarks to assess its own enrollment, employee salaries, and finances, as well as identify new opportunities for academic programs in promising industries.

Among many data markers for outcomes assessment, Trinity seeks to improve the overall 6-year graduation rate to a minimum of 55% by 2025. This is a stretch goal for a predominantly low-income student population. To evaluate this goal, the institution will look closely at first-year completion rate, based on attendance and passing grades; postgraduation employment; and the pass rate for licensure programs, such as certification in nursing (P. McGuire, personal interview, November 19, 2018). But administrators also carefully evaluate and celebrate in-course learning and incremental grade improvement as a measure of success, as well as students' development of personal strengths and soft skills.

Trinity measures fiscal success by its ability to maintain a balanced budget, meet debt covenants for building projects, and operate with a surplus while maintaining reserves and still providing an affordable education for its students. Throughout its transformation, the changes at Trinity have largely been possible through frugality: modest salaries and minimal infrastructure spending paired with strategic investments in technology and academic innovations. Even through its most financially challenging moments, Trinity did not freeze benefits or implement mass layoffs. Rather, by putting low-income students at the forefront of their work, administrators gained the support of local government, federal grants, and benefactors. Many of its students are Pell grant recipients and bring other outside scholarships to Trinity, which alleviates the cost per student. Once Trinity was designated a predominantly Black institution, it gained access to additional federal resources. The school has also conducted successful fundraising campaigns and received substantial grants from the Andrew W. Mellon Foundation and the Howard Hughes Medical Institute (Trinity Washington University, n.d.c). By rallying behind a compelling vision and strong leadership, remaining true to its mission, embracing change, and being willing to experiment and pivot, Trinity has repositioned itself firmly within the Integrated Model.

Figure 5.2. Trinity Washington University at a glance.

Endowment	$17 million
Student:Faculty Ratio	12:1
Enrollment	1,783
Four-Year Graduation Rate	20%
Six-Year Graduation Rate	44%
Key Elements of the Curriculum	General education curriculum emphasizes civic responsibility aligned with the liberal arts, honoring its tradition as a liberal arts Catholic college for women 40+ bachelor's and associate's degree programs across 12 disciplines Master's degrees offered in education, business and graduate studies, and professional studies

Trinity Washington University, n.d.b; U.S. Department of Education, 2019c.

6

UNDERSTANDING
THE DISTINCTIVE
PROGRAM MODEL

I n the last few decades there has been a growing body of research and
activity related to student learning in college. Campuses in the distinctive
program model seek to fully implement the aspects of this work that best
align with the campus mission and student interest, place these practices at
the center of all student work, and differentiate the institution based on that
vision.

In the 1990s Ernest Pascarella and Patrick Terenzini's (1991) *How
College Affects Students,* Alexander Astin's (1997) *What Matters in College,* and
Robert Barr and John Tagg's (1995) From Teaching to Learning to Learning
all shifted the discussion to focus more fully on student learning in college.
More recent research and national initiatives have built on this work and are
aimed at defining and strengthening liberal education while placing student
learning at the center of higher education (AAC&U, 2019; Kuh, O'Donnell,
Reed, 2013; Pascarella & Blaich, 2013). These efforts can reinforce the work
of small colleges. For example, a recent Gallup survey of college graduates
found that the two experiences that had the most lasting impact on students
after graduation were having a meaningful relationship with a faculty member
and participating in at least one form of engaged learning (Gallup-Purdue,
2014). Small colleges, with their intimate size, focus on the undergraduate
experience, and traditionally low student-to-faculty ratio, are well positioned
to offer such experiences. However, the rising costs associated with running
a residential campus often mean these experiences may happen incidentally
rather than by design. Lack of support and intentionality cedes what can be a
significant differentiator for small independent colleges, and can marginalize
a powerful form of student learning.

Institutions in the distinctive program model attempt to intentionally structure these important student experiences rather than leave them to chance. They proactively refocus the institution on implementing systems, infrastructure, and curriculum to emphasize those practices that have the greatest impact on student learning. They have committed to defining their education around a common student experience aligned with select best practices, ensuring ubiquity to promote student success.

Higher education scholars have identified a series of high-impact practices, so called because research has shown that these practices have a strong association with student learning and retention. These practices include first-year experiences, undergraduate research, service-learning, learning communities, internships, diversity and global learning, common intellectual experiences, collaborative learning, writing-intensive courses, and capstone projects (Kuh & Schneider, 2008). In addition, many institutions are adopting a program of integrative coaching or mentoring and are guiding their students in the development of digital portfolios. These efforts are designed to intentionally tie the student experience to life after college, responding to a changing student population that is more likely to be first generation and more concerned about the return on investment of a college education.

As research about, and knowledge of, high-impact practices has increased, the interest from campuses around the country has grown as well. One need only peruse the offerings of a current Council of Independent Colleges or AAC&U conference to see that these ideas have moved from research to implementation, and from the margins to the center of templates for student success (CIC, 2019b; AAC&U, 2019).

Many institutions have embraced the call for a greater emphasis on student learning by adding new programs or initiatives aimed at implementing some of these best practices. But crucially, at most campuses, such initiatives are additions to their regular curriculum and programs. By adding these initiatives as a new feature to their existing array of offerings, institutions essentially create a buffet of educational experiences from which students can choose, rather than ensuring they are a feature of every student's education.

While making high-impact practices another siloed and additional option may be an appropriate strategy for large universities or those with considerable resources, it is less effective at small colleges and universities. To implement these practices well requires considerable focus and discipline. If they are one more addition, it is difficult for most small colleges to find the financial or human capacity to support them with quality or at scale. The result, too often, is a number of poorly supported offices competing with other worthwhile endeavors for resources and students. They are high-impact practices in name, but the quality and scope of their implementation is often scattered and uncertain.

There are too many high-impact practices for any small college or university to adopt comprehensively as part of its distinctive program. The more successful approach, which we will see illustrated in profiles later in this chapter, involves identifying a subset of these experiences and designing them in a guided pathway for students. This ensures sufficient capacity for the campus to provide a common student experience that is both ubiquitous and delivered with quality.

It is important to note that the distinctive program model is different from finding a unique niche based on particular academic foci. An institution dedicated to infusing all courses with environmental concerns, such as College of the Atlantic, has a niche. The niche does not make them part of the distinctive program model, because the niche is built from a disciplinary approach. Distinctive program institutions are less concerned with specific disciplines, and focus instead on a common student learning experience regardless of academic discipline. Indeed, campuses in this group have migrated from both traditional liberal arts campuses and the integrated model. The important shift is not disciplinary, but moves from a disciplinary focus to a student learning focus.

Adopting the distinctive program model can substantially increase the quality of education while simultaneously differentiating the campus from other institutions. This makes it one of the most educationally promising, but one of the most institutionally challenging, routes to adaptation.

Consider that most small colleges and universities try to highlight why they are different (better) from other small colleges in their region or sector. Yet their own descriptions of their institutions employ phrases such as "personalized attention" or "small classes taught by full-time faculty," or "an education where we value the whole student"—phrases that appear with great frequency, across a multitude of institutions. While they do separate the institution from large research campuses, they do little more than that. One would be hard-pressed to determine which small college is associated with any of these statements, or even to distinguish the meaning of the phrases from each other. They are accurate, but benign and ultimately empty, descriptors of nearly every small college or university in the nation.

In contrast, campuses that adopt the distinctive program model have made a proactive and strategic decision to develop an educational experience that defines (marketers would say *brands*) the institution beyond such clichés. By making the needs of the contemporary student central and ensuring a specific set of high-impact practices are ubiquitous, the institution ties education to student success in college, in career, and in life. While continuing to embrace the centrality of small classes and personalized attention, these colleges and universities attempt to develop a more focused and institution-defining education.

Defining Features of the Distinctive Program Model

There are five defining features of the distinctive program model. First—and crucially—the program is ubiquitous. This means it is not simply another option for students in a buffet line but instead reaches every student. It also infuses their entire educational experience; it is more than a common first-year program or a common core. It is a comprehensive and intentional student learning experience that is central to students' curricular and cocurricular work. The ubiquity of the program is essential to its ability to positively influence student success and to elevate the campus and its identity to prospective students. As we will see in the accompanying profiles of campuses that have adopted this approach, the need for ubiquity is also a significant part of the challenge of implementation.

Second, the program is developed from research about best practices for student learning and is aligned with the needs of contemporary students, who are more likely to be first-generation college and from traditionally underrepresented groups. It is focused on student success, engagement, and pedagogy rather than specific disciplinary offerings. As one president remarked, it asks the campus to move from a program focus to a student success focus (E. Davis, personal interview, November 18, 2018).

Third, the program is market sensitive and market aware. It recognizes and responds to the needs of the contemporary student population by providing more clear pathways to career and to life beyond college than is typical of liberal arts institutions. Instead of relying only on specific disciplinary offerings to attract and retain students, the campus consciously links its distinctive program to success in college, in career, and in crafting a meaningful life.

Fourth, the program is mission-aligned. The goal of the distinctive program model is to embrace the institution's history and mission and adapt that mission to contemporary students. It evolves our notion of the liberal arts, rather than leaving behind the liberal arts core of the institution, and elevates what small colleges can, and should, do well: provide an intense focus on student success.

Fifth, the program is educationally sustainable. It is educationally sustainable through comprehensive integration into courses, curriculum, and cocurriculum, with appropriate campus expertise and assessment to embed it into ongoing practices. This is a major task, and as we will see in the institutional profiles, successful implementation requires considerable and ongoing attention.

Finally, the distinctive program model is also, ultimately, financially sustainable. If implemented thoroughly it can have a measurable and positive effect on enrollment, selectivity, retention, and persistence. It has as much or greater possibility for long-term financial stability as adding traditional, discrete, and market-driven academic programs, but its successful implementation requires the commitment and engagement of the entire institution.

Inherent Strengths of the Distinctive Program Model

The distinctive program model of institutional change has significant attractions for many campuses. If implemented with care and utilizing the processes of shared governance, it can capitalize on existing institutional strengths and history, while adapting them to the current realities. It is readily adoptable for institutions either in the traditional model or in the integrated model.

The challenges of demographic change, fiscal pressure, and expectations for employment-ready skills have many small colleges and universities questioning their core missions. The distinctive program approach allows an institution to retain fidelity to its mission and values but changes many of the ways in which they are delivered. It moves from a focus on disciplines and courses to a focus on student success and institutional sustainability, a move that allows ample space to embrace long-standing institutional values.

Most small colleges and universities do not have the resources or the expertise to continually expand services, programs, and educational delivery systems. The distinctive program model moves a campus from dispersing scarce resources across ever-expanding new programs and initiatives and instead invites core investment in student success built around a shared educational model. To be sure, campuses will still face competing requests and internal competition for resources; the distinctive program model clarifies and prioritizes these requests to align with the broader institutional vision.

One of the most compelling aspects of the distinctive program model is its ability to help an institution adapt to what we have seen is a rapidly changing student profile. This approach offers a significant opportunity to change in a way that more fully supports students and ties the educational experience to career and lifelong learning that is not discipline-specific. As we have seen, in the next few decades the only anticipated population growth in traditional-age students is in first-generation college students and in groups that have traditionally been underrepresented in higher education. These practices are tailored for student success and are effective for all student populations but provide a base for connectivity and responsiveness particularly necessary for the success of first-generation and underrepresented groups.

The distinctive program model also gives the campus the ability to clearly define its institutional identity. Instead of relying only on the usual tropes of small class size and personal relationships with faculty, colleges and universities can point to a distinctive student experience, one based on research and meaningful outcomes for students and their families. This allows the campus to refine its message and target outreach to students, as well as prospective faculty and prospective staff who share expertise and a passion for that mission.

Inherent Challenges of the Distinctive Program Model

The biggest challenge in fully adopting the distinctive program model is the degree of change it requires to fully and successfully implement. Moving a campus away from treating new programs as add-ons, and instead making an affirmative choice to elevate and centralize a common student experience, runs counter to the ways in which most of our institutions operate. There is often no natural internal constituency for such a shift—faculty are typically focused on building or preserving their disciplines and staff are usually accustomed to working in their discrete areas. Changing the institution to focus on a central, comprehensive approach to student learning and success requires a fundamental change to both systems and programs.

In adopting the distinctive program model, campuses must also carefully choose the right distinctive program, based on the institution's existing strengths. This means building internal support and engaging the board, alumni, and external constituencies; it also means having some clarity about the financial and student enrollment goals that should be the result of implementation. In the accompanying institutional profiles we will see that two campuses that adopted this approach also hired an external consultant to evaluate their current and prospective student market as the campus was generating ideas for its distinctive program approach. Investing in an idea that has limited support from the campus or broader constituencies, or has little interest to prospective students, can create conflict and marginalize the institution without bringing about needed change.

Finally, a program is not necessarily distinctive if every campus is adopting it. To ensure it is not only distinctive but differentiating requires a careful evaluation of institutional position, and an understanding of campuses with which the institution competes for students.

Contemporary Examples of the Distinctive Program Model

In recent years, the distinctive program model has gained currency as a means of transforming an institution while retaining fidelity to institutional mission. Colleges and universities that have implemented, or are in the process of adopting, the distinctive program model include Elon University (whose transformation is well chronicled in George Keller's (1994) book *Transforming a College*), Connecticut College, Hiram College, Queens University of Charlotte, Muskingum University, Chatham University, Mills College, Ohio Wesleyan University, and Marymount Manhattan College, among others. A fascinating example of a distinctive program approach that did not evolve from a long-standing liberal arts campus can be found at Kettering University.

In addition to these institutions, the accompanying campus profiles take a closer look at three institutions that have adopted the distinctive program model: Agnes Scott College, Dominican University of California (my own campus), and Furman University. These three campuses would not, at first glance, seem to have much in common. Agnes Scott is an undergraduate women's college located just outside of Atlanta, Georgia; Dominican is in California, formerly a women's and Catholic college that is now a coed and independent university Furman is a somewhat larger coed, undergraduate-focused institution in South Carolina. What aligns the three institutions, and what separates them from each other, is instructive for campuses considering the adoption of the distinctive program approach.

The campuses came to the distinctive program model from different positions in the small college framework. Dominican has both undergraduate and graduate programs and both liberal arts and professional programs, and was in the integrated model before adopting the distinctive program approach. Both Furman and Agnes Scott were in the traditional model of liberal arts colleges. All three were drawn to the distinctive program model to differentiate their campus and to strengthen the student experience both in and beyond college. Each recognized the need to adapt to changing student demographics while remaining committed to their core mission and identity. When considering the distinctive program approach, each was still suffering from the lingering effects of the 2008 recession.

To develop their distinctive programs, all of these campuses employed research about best practices in student learning to integrate the student experience and aligned that with recognition that the student population is becoming more diverse and contains more first-generation college-goers. As a result, they all developed programs that included a strong commitment to intentional mentoring or coaching, along with ongoing assessment. But each developed its own unique emphasis—for Agnes Scott it is global leadership, for Dominican it is community engagement and signature work, for Furman it is a guided pathway that emphasizes engaged learning.

All three of these campuses worked fully within the existing strengths of the institution and remained committed to a rigorous shared governance process to achieve a shared understanding of the program, its goals, and its implementation. In each case, substantial curriculum revision, faculty and staff development, and systems changes were necessary. And each shares a commitment to becoming student centered, rather than program centered, tying the student experience to integrate work in and out of the classroom and to life beyond college.

But there are also substantial differences in the campuses and their process of adopting the distinctive program model. Most notable is the difference in campus wealth (or lack of it), and subsequent ability to invest in the transformation to a distinctive program approach. Furman, as a Duke Endowment institution, was able to put significant funds into the program almost from its inception. Agnes Scott used a combination of a special endowment draw, fundraising, and board support, understanding that at least part of the endowment draw would be repaid over time. Dominican's modest endowment did not provide the capacity for a special endowment draw, and the campus instead has relied on the extraordinary generosity of key board members, as well as important first-time gifts from major national foundations. The fact that each was able to achieve successful implementation speaks to the validity of the approach and the importance of engaged shared governance in its execution.

PROFILE OF A DISTINCTIVE PROGRAM MODEL INSTITUTION: AGNES SCOTT COLLEGE

Field research and draft compilation of this campus profile conducted by Todd J. Denning while an EdM student at the Harvard Graduate School of Education

The charming Metropolitan Atlanta city of Decatur, Georgia, is home to Agnes Scott College, an independent women's college known for its innovative liberal arts curriculum. Founded in 1889 as Decatur Female Seminary, the college is listed on the National Register of Historic Places as part of the South Candler Street–Agnes Scott College Historic District. A walk around campus reveals sprawling green lawns and architecture reminiscent of elite New England institutions, and the institution's mascot, the Scottie dog, adds even more charm. Student pride runs deep and is a clear cultural aspect of the student experience, and the institution channels this pride and its core values into a distinct identity.

The college's published mission is to "educate women to think deeply, live honorably and engage the intellectual and social challenges of their times" (Agnes Scott College, n.d.b). Its enrollment is just over 1,000. Enrollment has recently been growing and is at an all-time high; the class of 2022 is the largest in the institution's history. As we will see, much of this increase can be traced to the adoption of a distinctive program model of institutional innovation, aptly named SUMMIT. Although Agnes Scott has enjoyed growing visibility in recent years and is classified as a national liberal arts college, approximately half of its students still hail from Georgia. Its student population is diverse. Thirteen percent of its students identify as Hispanic/Latina, 31% identity as Black or African American, 7% identify as Asian, 6% identify as multiracial, and 7% are international; 41% of students receive Pell grants; and about 15% of students are in the first generation in their family to attend college.

Agnes Scott offers programs in 34 majors and 31 minors, the most popular of which include business management, English literature–creative writing, history, neuroscience, psychology, and public health. The 4- and 6-year graduation rates are 67% and 69%, respectively, and the first-year retention rate is 83% based on an average of the past 3 years. The institution has a student-to-faculty ratio of 10:1.

Two New Initiatives

Like many small institutions with enrollment challenges, Agnes Scott sought ways to innovate its curriculum while also leveraging its strengths in the process. Agnes Scott tackled misperceptions of the liberal arts head-on by adding changes to the curriculum and cocurriculum, such as infusing it with leadership development and global learning. This is more than a simple repackaging of the long-established liberal arts curriculum.

President Leocadia "Lee" Zak assumed the role of president of Agnes Scott in July 2018 and inherited the structure of the SUMMIT innovations. When asked about what drew her to Agnes Scott, she cites her experience as a student at Mount Holyoke College, a women's liberal arts college in Massachusetts. As an avid proponent for women's colleges, she emphasizes the power of community and the unique learning environment these institutions provide to their students. President Zak explained that Agnes Scott has implemented two major initiatives in response to the challenges facing small colleges. The first and most visible transformation was the launch of a new initiative intended to reinvigorate and add new relevance to the liberal arts. SUMMIT is meant to embody the Agnes Scott experience and is designed to prepare students to be effective change agents in a global society. In this reimagined liberal arts education, every student completes a course of study along with cocurricular experiences, that develop leadership abilities and an understanding of complex global dynamics.

Agnes Scott has long been known for combining a rigorous liberal arts curriculum with intentional global learning opportunities, and its mission statement articulates the importance of developing leadership skills. SUMMIT was designed to build on these strengths and ensure all students benefit from an integrated experience. The interdisciplinary themes of the curriculum are leadership development and global learning, which are supported by a board of advisers for each student, along with a digital portfolio. Students may choose to specialize in either leadership development or global learning, although all students are required to take foundational coursework related to both areas. More specifically, students start their first semester with a two-day experiential leadership immersion. This is followed by a required course within a discipline highlighting leadership as a process of reflecting on individual strengths, identity, and power; analyzing evidence, perspectives, and systems; and acting authentically, boldly, and ethically. In addition to these requirements in leadership development, every first-year student participates in a required spring Global Journeys course that integrates classroom learning and firsthand experience of complex global dynamics in a weeklong global immersion experience. The institution makes a point to lead with this experience to allow future discussions on global dynamics to draw from it. Students are placed in 1 of 16 Journeys classes, cohorts of about 20 students each, adding a further level of quality to the program as an individual student will often have an entirely different experience from her peers, depending on her journey. The various Journeys classes share common readings that can be understood in these individual contexts.

In addition to the curriculum, students are supported throughout their time at Agnes Scott by a board of advisers that includes a SUMMIT adviser, peer advising, career advising, and a major adviser. The SUMMIT adviser and major adviser are the backbone of student mentorship, but each of the four advisers has an important role to play at different stages of a student's undergraduate experience. Students can seek many different types of support, including academic and professional, from these advisers. Figure 6.1 provides an illustration of the SUMMIT program.

Over the course of four years, in addition to the traditional liberal arts skills of writing, public speaking, and critical thinking, students develop teamwork skills and twenty-first-century digital competencies (in areas

Figure 6.1. Illustration of the SUMMIT program.

SUMMIT: THE AGNES SCOTT COLLEGE EXPERIENCE

LEADERSHIP DEVELOPMENT

All Agnes Scott students complete coursework and experiences focused on the acquisition of five essential leadership skills—critical thinking, writing, public speaking, teamwork and digital literacy—and reflect on what it means to be an honorable leader.

Those who elect to complete the Leadership Development Specialization augment this foundational work with a personalized slate of courses in Leadership Studies, practical leadership experiences and additional skills development. Completion of the specialization is noted on their transcript.

GLOBAL LEARNING

Every Agnes Scott student completes introductory course work and a faculty-led study tour focused on understanding complex global dynamics.

Students who elect to complete the Global Learning Specialization further hone their understanding of global structures, systems and processes through advanced course work and immersion experiences, leading to a notation on their transcript.

BOARD OF ADVISORS

As students blaze their unique paths to the SUMMIT, they benefit from the expertise of not just one, but four advisors—a SUMMIT Advisor, a Peer Advisor, a Major Advisor and a Career Ally.

DIGITAL PORTFOLIO

A self-curated virtual space in which students collect artifacts from, reflect upon and showcase selected aspects of their unique learning journey.

Note: Agnes Scott College (2019).

including digital communication, visual literacy, and information literacy, among others) as they use their portfolio to catalog digital evidence of the most salient aspects of their SUMMIT experience. In the senior year, every student completes a required capstone course where they critically examine their digital identity and curate the contents of their digital portfolio to tell their personal story to a public audience. President Zak describes these portfolios as "very impressive" and lauds the students' ability to create appealing and professional virtual spaces. Channeling their design-oriented and social-media skills into professional platforms is one of the ways Scotties (how students at Agnes Scott refer to themselves) leverage SUMMIT in order to prepare for life after graduation.

The second response to the changing landscape of higher education was the launch of new programs at the graduate level in 2018. The college had discontinued its master of arts in teaching programs in 2010. Among a suite of new graduate programs, the first program to launch was Writing and Digital Communications. Other programs beginning in 2019 include Evaluation and Assessment Methods, Applied Technology, Data Visualization, and Social Innovation. As was true for the development of SUMMIT, the establishment of these graduate programs was data driven and incorporated strengths already held by Agnes Scott. This process included an assessment of the trajectory of higher education, and then the identification of what was feasible, yet meaningful, to implement.

Process and Implementation

The teaching of the liberal arts, according to President Zak, is an area in which Agnes Scott has always maintained institutional strength. Indeed, SUMMIT's development was carefully choreographed with the expertise and leadership of faculty, many of whom made it their mission to ensure that it was authentic and met the goals set out for it. This accountability for quality on behalf of the faculty is what has allowed Agnes Scott to adapt and evolve when necessary.

The higher education consulting firm Art & Science Group was engaged to collect data on growth trends, and interviews with inquiring and admitted students were used to target what prospective students desired most from their education. The result was a framework for creating SUMMIT, and the institution's leadership continued to build on this framework in order to quickly move the consensus-building process. This process of determining what the initiative needed and establishing specific goals took about two years and centered on shared governance. With the framework for SUMMIT underway, the academic curriculum needed to be modified, and faculty worked to incorporate themes of leadership development and global learning into their courses. This was a significant undertaking that took 18 months to complete. President Zak points to the common understanding among faculty, staff, administrators, and the board of trustees of the urgency for the college to make such changes. Fueled by growing concerns about the future of small liberal arts colleges, especially women's colleges, Agnes Scott began to focus its efforts on translating the consulting insight it received into a new and innovative curriculum.

Today, for example, courses in philosophy ask students questions such as, "What does Plato have to say about leadership, and why is this relevant?"

This process of incorporating leadership development and global learning into the curriculum, according to some faculty members, was not seamless for all courses. Some disciplines required a greater level of effort in weaving leadership development and global learning into their curricula, but significant progress has been made in understanding how faculty can adapt their pedagogies to complement the institution's focus on leadership and global issues.

Financing the Transformation

Agnes Scott has had success in finding ways to fund SUMMIT. Financial support for the new initiative has been achieved through a combination of fundraising, especially for the Journeys, and an investment by the board of trustees through a special draw from the endowment. The institution has a $230 million endowment, solid for the size of the institution, but about half that of other similarly ranked schools (Agnes Scott College, n.d.a). The endowment helps to support SUMMIT, but it is not the only means by which SUMMIT will be sustainably supported.

President Zak attributes the excitement and satisfaction with the experience by students as the primary reason for success in funding it. The draw from the endowment is carefully monitored in order to ensure that it is being used for the sole purpose of providing the best experience possible for students, many of whom define their Agnes Scott experience by their innovative liberal arts education. Financial support from the endowment is temporary, and measures of success to determine adequate return on investment are employed with the goal of the operating budget eventually supporting SUMMIT in full. Measures of success that are on track include application growth, admitted student yield, enrollment growth, strength of the incoming class, average family income, and net tuition revenue.

A clear goal for SUMMIT is to be self-sustaining and remain a vehicle for Agnes Scott's growth; the promising future for SUMMIT is evident in its success to date, and more specific actions will be taken to assess the outcomes of graduates.

Outcomes and Assessment

President Zak describes SUMMIT and the institution's new graduate programs as transformative. SUMMIT has contributed to the institution's reputation as an innovative place for learning in the liberal arts. In 2018, *U.S.*

News & World Report placed Agnes Scott in the #1 spot of its list of the most innovative liberal arts colleges (Agnes Scott College, 2018).

A survey given to the class of 2022 asked students to identify what was most important to them when deciding to attend Agnes Scott; 95% indicated that SUMMIT was either "important" or "very important" in informing their decision to enroll. This extraordinary figure points to SUMMIT's ability to cut through the noise of the narrative normally told to prospective students about the value of a liberal arts education. Effective marketing, the clear goals of the program, and the possibility of better outcomes for graduates gives SUMMIT an unprecedented level of visibility to prospective students and their families, addressing a challenge all too familiar to many small colleges.

While SUMMIT's initial framework remains intact, the college isn't afraid to make necessary changes for the betterment of the student experience. After all, President Zak describes SUMMIT as unique because it is more than a curriculum—it is the embodiment of student life. The class of 2019 will be the first graduating class to have experienced SUMMIT for a full four years. The postgraduation outcomes of these students will be monitored carefully, and President Zak mentions the importance of surveys in the collection of critical data. These data will be used to assess what is and is not

Figure 6.2. Agnes Scott College at a glance.

Endowment	$230 million
Student-to-Faculty Ratio	10:1
Enrollment	1,040
Four-Year Graduation Rate	67%
Six-Year Graduation Rate	69%
Key Elements of the Curriculum	Distinctive student experience: SUMMIT program Curriculum supports traditional liberal arts skills development and twenty-first-century digital competencies 34 majors Bachelor's and master's degrees are offered, as well as postbaccalaureate premedical program

Note: U.S. Department of Education (2017a).

working and could highlight room for growth and further innovation. Of course, other types of surveys, such as satisfaction surveys, have been used during the past few years to provide perspective on how the initiative is faring according to students. SUMMIT's innovation is designed to be continuous and is a regular part of ensuring its ongoing success.

PROFILE OF A DISTINCTIVE PROGRAM MODEL INSTITUTION: DOMINICAN UNIVERSITY OF CALIFORNIA

This profile was written by Jennifer M. Krengel, M.A.

Since its founding by the Dominican Sisters of San Rafael in 1890, Dominican University of California has had a long tradition of adapting to a changing society while maintaining its commitment to academic excellence and student support. Originally established as a women's college, Dominican became the first Catholic institution in California to grant the Bachelor of Arts degree to women in 1917 and, in 1924, the California teaching credential (Barry & Barry, 1984). This marked the beginning of a period of growth into new fields of study, an increase in the number and diversity of faculty and students, and an expansion of the physical campus. Through an early academic partnership with Catholic University of America, Dominican began offering graduate courses in education, English, French, and history in 1950 (Barry & Barry, 1984).

Dominican became an independent university in 1969, when the college's ownership and operation transitioned entirely to a lay board of trustees. In another major change, recognizing "the need for continued modernization of the curriculum in harmony with changing society," the institution became fully coeducational in 1971 (Barry & Barry, 1984). Over the next three decades, academic offerings evolved to support internationalization and expansion into professional programs. In 2000, the college became Dominican University of California.

Today, the university serves nearly 1,800 graduate and undergraduate students. It remains committed to the Dominican values of study, reflection, community, and service. The university offers nearly 40 programs that integrate the liberal arts, sciences, and professional study. Dominican's student profile is highly diverse. Seventy-one percent of students identify as ethnically diverse, most from groups underrepresented in higher education; 31% are Pell-eligible, and 22% are from the first generation in their family to attend college (M. Nicklasson, personal communication, March 18, 2019). In recent years, the university has focused on increasing retention, building academic quality, and adding new programs in areas of strength, all to support an increasingly diverse student population. At the heart of institutional transformation is the creation of the Dominican Experience for all, a signature educational model committed to the flourishing of every student.

Strategic Planning and the Dominican Experience

In 2011 Mary B. Marcy began her tenure as Dominican's ninth president at a time when the university was attempting considerable expansion in enrollment, both through online and on-campus degree completion programs (N. Pitchford, personal interview, March 21, 2019). However, this expansion had not always been sustainable or supported, resulting in unpredictable budgets and concerns about student success. In 2011, the 4-year graduation rate at Dominican was 34%, the 6-year rate was 49%, and the campus was facing significant budget cuts.

The institution had recently adopted the 2011–2015 Strategic Plan. The plan was broad, encompassing 9 central categories that contained a total of 25 initiatives, and in retrospect, highlighted the challenge with overly prescriptive and sometimes competing goals (Dominican University of California, 2017). Nevertheless, the plan did include a commitment to academic quality and student support. Evaluating the plan along with data on Dominican's graduation and retention rates, current and likely future student demographics, and research on best practices that support student success, President Marcy engaged the campus in a comprehensive planning process that focused on the initiatives that were truly strategic, academic in nature, and university wide.

In 2013–2014, a sizeable planning group comprising faculty, staff, and students was established to evaluate six topics that would inform the evolution of Dominican's strategic plan: curriculum, partnerships, faculty/staff roles and rewards, data infrastructure, physical campus, and the Dominican Experience. Each task force addressed planning questions while utilizing national research about student learning, as well as evaluating the projections about demographic and economic challenges to higher education. Central to the planning process were a number of forums, which included presidential listenings (gatherings at the president's residence on a particular topic) and campus-wide retreats designed to facilitate dialogue across disciplines and faculty and staff groupings. Outside experts were brought in to help frame planning discussions; however, much of the visioning work was led by the campus. The process produced a vision for the Dominican Experience, which articulated a signature student experience that built on existing institutional strengths.

In summer 2014, a team of faculty, staff, and administrators attended the AAC&U Summer Institute on High-Impact Practices and Student Success. The institute focused on improving completion rates and quality of student learning, as well as removing barriers to student success (AAC&U, 2014). These discussions informed and helped further refine the vision for the Dominican Experience. The institute provided access to emerging research, as well as professional development for those who would lead implementation of the Dominican Experience on campus.

This signature student experience, which places Dominican firmly in the distinctive program model, promises that all students, regardless of proclivity or major areas of study, will receive similar support, tools, and experiences with which to succeed (Dominican University of California, 2017). The Dominican Experience comprises four signature components: integrative coaching and mentorship, development of a digital portfolio, community engagement, and signature work (Figure 6.3).

Figure 6.3. The four components of the Dominican Experience.

THE DOMINICAN EXPERIENCE

Integrative Coaching:
Students work with an integrative coach and a network of mentors throughout their undergraduate careers.

Signature Work:
Students complete signature work such as a research project, a giant mural, or a business plan.

Community Engagement:
Students engage with the community through service-learning, internships, fieldwork, community-based research, or global learning.

Digital Portfolio:
Students craft a digital portfolio that captures the journey and assists in the transition to career or graduate school.

Note: Dominican University of California (2019).

Integrative Coaching and Mentoring

The integrative coaching and Mentoring component complements the existing advising structure within academic departments and expands the scope of Dominican's Academic Advising and Achievement Center. In addition to the faculty adviser, this model matches students with an integrative coach, peer mentor, and career mentor, connecting students with those who can consistently support and guide them as their needs and aspirations evolve. As the primary relationship in this model, the integrative coach serves as a touchstone throughout students' time on campus, helping them develop education and career plans, guiding the use of digital portfolios, facilitating peer and career mentor relationships, and reinforcing institutional learning outcomes. Integrative coaches also teach two courses that make up the coaching curriculum: Mastering College in the first year, and Life Skills 101 in the third or fourth year (Dominican University of California, 2017).

Peer mentors are trained sophomore, junior, and senior Dominican students who partner with incoming students to help them make connections on campus and in the community and assist new students as they create their digital portfolios. Career mentors are professionals and alumni who provide guidance as students prepare for future work and graduate programs.

This component of the Dominican Experience is designed to increase students' persistence through graduation and to support their life beyond the university. Research suggests that students are two times more likely to be engaged at their work postgraduation if they had a mentor in college who encouraged them to pursue their goals (Gallup-Purdue, 2014).

Digital Portfolio

Each student's development of a digital portfolio begins within the integrative coaching model. Incoming students are trained by peer mentors to design digital portfolios that they will share with their faculty advisers. Digital portfolios are integrated into general education and throughout the major in order to capture students' learning and reflections over time. Personal education plans, career plans, and signature work are all housed within the portfolio. Dominican's portfolio also contains a tab for institutional learning outcomes, enabling students to organize their work and make the value and demonstration of skills more visible for graduate school applications, prospective employers, and students themselves (Dominican University of California, 2017).

Community Engagement

The community engagement component of the Dominican Experience reflects the university's long-standing commitment to community and service. It is broad by design, encompassing service-learning, global learning, internships, clinical placements and fieldwork, project-based learning and teamwork, and community-based research. Prior to establishing the Dominican Experience, these high-impact learning experiences were often isolated by program. By creating an institutional framework that recognizes the range of community-engaged learning at Dominican, these practices are aligned to create a more inclusive and coherent narrative of this work.

Along with increasing student learning and enhancing the likelihood of student success in college, this component of the Dominican Experience draws on research conducted for AAC&U. This research revealed that employers are 69% more likely to hire a student who had completed a community-based project (AAC&U, 2015).

Signature Work

The Dominican Experience culminates in the creation of each student's signature work, intended to reflect a work of substance, created over a period of time, and driven by a student's own inquiry (Dominican University of California, 2017). Students begin by identifying a question of interest and are guided by faculty and mentors as they prepare, for example, a research paper, policy brief, choreographed dance, painting, or business plan. Students often elect to share signature work on their digital portfolio and on Dominican Scholar, an online repository of original work created by students, faculty, and staff of the institution. Since 2014, the annual Scholarly and Creative Works Conference has also been a venue for sharing and celebrating students' signature work with the campus and the broader community.

This aspect of the Dominican Experience is also correlated with student success after college: 73% of employers believe college students should be required to complete a significant applied learning project (AAC&U, 2015).

To some degree, the four components of the Dominican Experience existed on campus prior to 2014. However, these practices were isolated to a handful of programs, were not always well developed or adequately supported, and were far from evenly distributed amongst students.

Ashley Finley, who served as dean for the Dominican Experience 2015–2018, recognizes that these high-impact learning experiences are beneficial for all students and saw the program as a pathway to providing greater equity and support across the highly diverse student population. First-generation and underrepresented students often hesitate to pursue experiences they perceive will delay time to degree. The Dominican Experience model is particularly effective in supporting a diverse student population partly because its components are, by design, ubiquitous. By embedding the four components into the curriculum and cocurriculum, the Dominican Experience promises equitable access to the most effective resources and experiences that support high-impact learning for every student (A. Finley, personal interview, March 28, 2019).

Learning Outcomes and Curriculum Transformation

In order to ensure the Dominican Experience was embedded across all programs and to provide intentional, holistic support for an increasingly diverse student body, the institution realized the curriculum needed to adapt as well. Through a highly collaborative process, faculty and staff defined a common set of outcomes that reinforce the Dominican Experience and construct a framework for assessment. These outcomes were approved by the faculty forum and the staff assembly in spring 2016. This work provided momentum and laid the groundwork for an ambitious revision of the university's entire curriculum.

The following academic year, curriculum revision was fully underway. In December 2017, faculty voted by a majority of 85% to transform Dominican's general education program, shifting away from a pathway focused on specific academic disciplines to a core curriculum defined by skills and competencies that align with the Dominican Experience. The total general education requirements for graduation were reduced from 45 units to 36 units, in order to provide greater responsiveness to student exploration, while streamlining time to degree and addressing the unsustainable 9:1 student-to-faculty ratio.

In spring 2018, the faculty then turned its attention to curriculum change in the majors and minors. In just 4 months, the faculty revised 23 majors, 16 minors, and 7 graduate programs. Each proposal received a nearly unanimous vote of support from the faculty, approval from the president's cabinet, and a unanimous vote of approval and acclamation from the board of trustees. Much of this work was accomplished through collaboration across programs, resulting in greater interdisciplinarity within the newly constituted majors.

President Marcy notes the revised curriculum has three measurable and important outcomes that support the institution's financial health and commitment to quality. First, it provides greater relevance and a clearer path to degree for students. Second, it reduces faculty workload. Third, by increasing the student-to-faculty ratio from an unsustainable 9:1 to a manageable 14:1, it lowers costs while maintaining the university's commitment to personalized education.

Defining the Institution and Inviting Innovation

The Dominican Experience established a new vocabulary for defining *student success* and created a common narrative about institutional strengths. It has also supported significant gains in retention and persistence and is now the primary framework for evaluating new strategic partnerships. Messaging about the Dominican Experience has become central to admission efforts and external communications, which have elevated the university's profile and recognition as an innovative institution.

Retention and Persistence

As the university has worked to implement the Dominican Experience and curricular change, it has maintained focused attention on increasing student retention and graduation rates. Over the 7-year period between 2011 and 2018, Dominican's 4-year graduation rates have increased dramatically, from 34% to 58%; similarly, 6-year graduation rates have increased from 49% to 73% in that same time period. Retention rates have seen a significant improvement as well. First-to second-year undergraduate retention increased from 69% in 2007 to 82% in 2018 (M. Nicklasson, personal communication, March 20, 2019).

New Strategic Partnerships

For small, independent institutions like Dominican, President Marcy notes the importance of continuing to adapt and innovate and says the Dominican Experience has served as a central framework against which to evaluate new and innovative partnerships (personal interview, March 26, 2019). One such partnership is with Make School, a Bay Area computer science training provider. Through an incubation relationship that received approval from regional accreditor WSCUC in fall 2018, the partnership is enabling Dominican to establish an applied computer science minor available to all undergraduate students and enabling Make School to offer an accelerated bachelor's degree in applied computer science. Central to the ability to create the partnership was Make School's embrace of the four components of the Dominican Experience (more details of this partnership can be found in chapter 10).

Another partnership that was made possible through the Dominican Experience is Reimagining Citizenship, which the university launched in fall 2018 in collaboration with the city of Novato. In this unique scholarship program, students receive a college education while engaging with the community through local government. Under the terms of the partnership, the neighboring city of Novato and Dominican select a cohort of students to become Reimagining Citizenship Fellows. Students selected through a competitive process receive paid summer work with the city before they begin college, and again between their first and second year of college. In turn, Dominican provides a substantial scholarship, offers targeted support and mentorship for the Reimagining Citizenship cohort, and grants the students credit toward a minor in community action and social change.

Enhanced Visibility and Enrollment

As the Dominican Experience, curriculum revision, and innovative new partnerships have moved from conception to implementation, the university has been able to elevate its visibility. During the 2018–2019 academic year, a number of faculty, staff, students, and senior leaders presented on the topics of curricular revision, integrative coaching, innovation in higher education, and emerging results of the Dominican Experience at conferences in the United States and abroad. Dominican's approach to innovation resulted in national media coverage unusual for a small campus, including features in the *Washington Post, Wall Street Journal, Chronicle of Higher Education*, and *Inside Higher Education.* Not all stories have directly referred to the Dominican Experience; however, they tend to reflect a cohesive narrative about the institution's identity and approach to innovation that is anchored by this distinctive program.

Outreach and marketing materials were revised to fully integrate messaging about the Dominican Experience for the fall 2018 admissions cycle. These marketing efforts aligned with the increased visibility and are having a positive influence on the size and selectivity of enrollment. In 2018 the university saw a 20% increase in the entering class, and a year later, enrollment numbers continued to increase (M. Marcy, personal interview, April 15, 2019).

Planning and Sustainability

Dominican does not have a large endowment from which to draw; therefore, fundraising has been essential to support the creation and initial implementation of the Dominican Experience. Leadership gifts from members of the board of trustees and major donors have played a key role in developing the coaching and mentoring component of the experience and are providing the resources to create a dedicated physical space, the Center for the Dominican Experience. Philanthropic investment was also secured from the Mellon Foundation, enabling the university to establish an inaugural deanship for the Dominican Experience. Additional funding from the Arthur Vining Davis Foundations has supported ongoing professional development for faculty and staff, and strategic budget reallocation has supported program development (M. Marcy, personal interview, March 26, 2019).

Nicola Pitchford, vice president for academic affairs and dean of the faculty, indicates that bringing the Dominican Experience fully to scale has required realignment of resources to ensure adequate support for the 4 components. The university's current strategic plan, titled Dominican at 130 (as the institution will be 130 years old in 2021), illustrates the interaction among 3 strategic categories: the Dominican Experience, curriculum alignment, and enrollment management. The plan provides benchmarks against which to measure success and has enabled the campus to simultaneously focus on actions that support a quality educational experience and the long-term financial health of the institution (N. Pitchford, personal interview, March 21, 2019).

Conclusion

The multifaceted nature of Dominican's approach to innovation belies the institution's commitment to structured, systemic, sustainable change. Each new initiative, from the launch of a partnership with Make School to the transformation of the institution's entire curriculum, draws inspiration from the Dominican Experience: a foundational set of principles and programs designed to address the challenges and realize the potential of a new generation of students. In turn, the Dominican Experience draws on the university's mission, values, and existing strengths. Improvements in student outcomes over the past seven years, curricular overhaul, new partnerships, commitment to citizenship and community engagement, focus on student success, and financial equilibrium have yielded tangible results in the present and position the university well for the future.

Figure 6.4. Dominican University of California at a glance.

Endowment	$33 Million
Student-to-Faculty Ratio	9:1
Enrollment	1,746
Four-Year Graduation Rate	58%
Six-Year Graduation Rate	72.8%
Key Elements of the Curriculum	The Dominican Experience Liberal arts, health and natural sciences, business

Dominican University of California Institutional Research, 2019; U.S. Department of Education, 2017b.

PROFILE OF A DISTINCTIVE PROGRAM MODEL INSTITUTION: FURMAN UNIVERSITY

Field research and draft compilation of this campus profile conducted by Andrew Marshall while an EdM student at the Harvard Graduate School of Education

Furman University occupies more than 700 acres in Greenville, South Carolina. Founded in 1826, the university enrolls just over 2,700 undergraduate students, along with 200 graduate students. Offering more than 60 areas of study and an 11:1 student-to-faculty ratio, Furman at first glance embodies the traditional liberal arts campus (U.S. Department of Education, 2017c). However, through the relatively recent commitment to develop a distinctive student experience, known as the Furman Advantage, the university is differentiating itself from these traditional peers.

The Furman Advantage

The Furman Advantage, launched in fall 2016, "guarantees every student an unparalleled education that combines classroom learning with real-world experiences and self-discovery" (Furman University, n.d.). Every student who attends Furman is guaranteed access to an engaged learning experience along with guidance from mentors, building the skills to connect their education to their career (E. Davis, personal interview, November 18, 2018).

The program is laid out as an integrated four-year program (Furman University, n.d.). Beginning in the first year, students are exposed to a robust mentoring and advising program that evolves throughout their time at Furman. Still in development, when fully launched the two-year, for-credit

Pathways advising program will ensure regular adviser-student engagement with developmentally appropriate curriculum that helps students leverage the whole of their college experience (E. Davis, personal interview, November 18, 2018; M. Horhota, personal interview, December 14, 2018).

The first-year curriculum focuses on transitioning to college and exploring students' values, identity, and interests. It provides students with skills to engage in intentional reflection and sets the foundation for development of a meaningful four-year plan at Furman. In the second year, these advising conversations begin to center around the selection of a major and look ahead toward an engaged learning experience. Students conduct informational interviews with alumni to learn more about potential career paths. These connections are made, and the interactions traced, through a curated database system. The system coordinates opportunities offered through the Pathways program and also tracks opportunities offered through the internship office and the Malone Center for Career Engagement. Optimally slotted into the third-year, the engaged learning experience is most commonly a study away experience, internship, or undergraduate research or creative project (Furman University, n.d.).

Classes, mentoring, and advising continue in the third and fourth years, as academic departments partner with offices across campus to offer tailored experiences to their majors related to applying to graduate schools and careers in their disciplines. The focus begins shifting to the future, synthesizing the experiences each student has moved through and beginning to connect them to next steps (M. Horhota, personal interview, December 14, 2018).

This four-year model, the Furman Advantage (Figure 6.5), is centered on the concept of reflection. Philosopher and education reformer John Dewey (1933) said, "We do not learn from experience . . . we learn from reflecting on experience," and his insight is integrated throughout the Furman Advantage (Dewey; p. 78 quoted by C. Carson, personal interview, December 14, 2018). Reflection, at its core, asks students to tie together the whole of their educational experience. It asks students to consider what aspects of their education have been most meaningful and valuable. Finally, it invites students to integrate these themes and incorporate them into a vision for life and career after college (Furman University, n.d.; M. Horhota, personal interview, December 14, 2018).

The goal is not only to reflect but also to develop the habit of reflection, so that it becomes a natural part of students' processing of experience. To aid in this habit-building, faculty and staff regularly participate in professional development workshops on reflective practices. Additionally, Furman added a Reflection Fellow to its internal Faculty Development Center to

Figure 6.5. Illustration of the Furman Advantage.

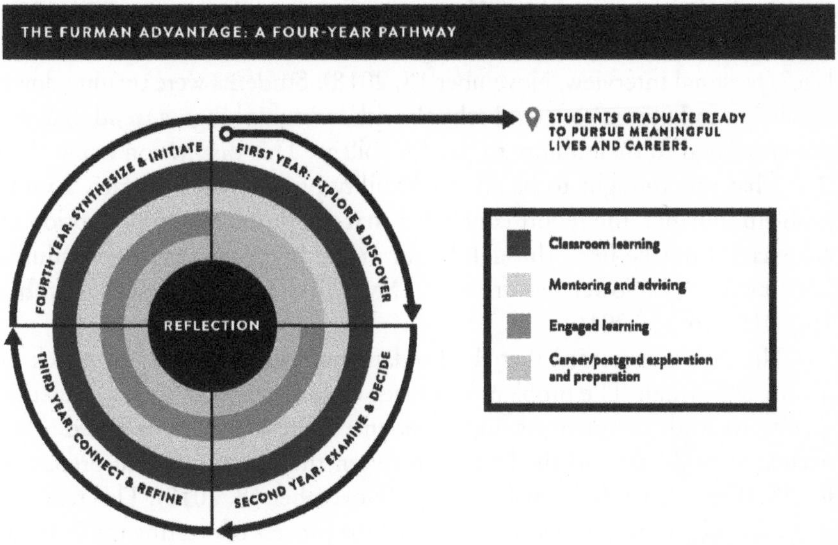

THE FURMAN ADVANTAGE: A FOUR-YEAR PATHWAY

STUDENTS GRADUATE READY TO PURSUE MEANINGFUL LIVES AND CAREERS.

FIRST YEAR: EXPLORE & DISCOVER

SECOND YEAR: EXAMINE & DECIDE

THIRD YEAR: CONNECT & REFINE

FOURTH YEAR: SYNTHESIZE & INITIATE

REFLECTION

Classroom learning

Mentoring and advising

Engaged learning

Career/postgrad exploration and preparation

Furman University (n.d.).

make resources on reflective practices available and standardize the language around reflection on campus (Furman University, n.d.; M. Horhota, personal interview, December 14, 2018).

Starting With a Vision

President Elizabeth Davis joined Furman in July of 2014. The 2008 financial crisis had changed the landscape for many liberal arts colleges, including Furman. Student enrollment yield was dropping, while the acceptance rate and discount rate increased. Furman was not attracting the students it once did (E. Davis, personal interview, November 18, 2018; Kovacs, 2016).

While the board of trustees had already expressed interest in developing some type of program that would differentiate the university, it was up to the new president to understand the strengths of the campus and build a vision. One of the first things President Davis did was retain the consulting firm Art & Science Group to conduct a comprehensive market positioning analysis of Furman. The declining enrollment metrics (e.g., yield, acceptance rate, retention) were not fully explainable through internal assessment alone and begged for an informed external analysis (E. Davis, personal interview, November 18, 2018).

The results of the Art & Science marketing study confirmed that Furman had a value problem. The report found, in the words of President Davis, that "essentially we were a regional, undifferentiated liberal arts college" (personal interview, November 18, 2018). Students were turning down admission to Furman to attend schools with lower rankings, a trend that was not correlated to their ability to pay for college. This distinction made clear that what was thought to be an affordability problem was, in fact, a value problem. Further, the report concluded that the problem and perception of value could not be fixed through better marketing, more aggressive admissions tactics, or a lower net price (E. Davis, personal interview, November 18, 2018; Kovacs, 2016).

The report indicated that the fundamental problem was not a lack of quality at Furman. The problem was a lack of connection of strong academic quality to student outcomes and experiences. President Davis noted, "We needed to build around the balance between the liberal arts and preparing for life after college" (personal interview, November 18, 2018). This research and subsequent campus discussion started the process of creating the Furman Advantage.

It is apparent from interviews and reviewing the process of creating the Furman Advantage that the goal was to engage the campus and to build on nascent institutional strengths. As President Davis stated, "We wanted to be able to capture everyone's imaginations, as opposed to saying it had to be done like this." (personal interview, November 18, 2018). That effort began with a straightforward vision to guarantee every student the chance to integrate their curricular and cocurricular work and to have a team of mentors that would connect campus experiences to work and life after college.

President Davis took that vision and worked with a small group of faculty to create a white paper to begin to outline what a new plan for student engagement could look like. The white paper was presented to faculty chairs, and then the faculty at large, in the 2015–2016 academic year (E. Davis, personal interview, November 18, 2018).

Having established the basic concept that would ultimately become the Furman Advantage, the process then moved to a Strategic Vision Advisory Council. The council was cochaired by then-Interim Dean of the Faculty Ken Peterson, a long-serving member of the faculty, and Vice President for Student Life Connie Carson. The council worked through the summer of 2016, a process President Davis called "critical to the design," as it modelled close collaboration between academic affairs and student affairs to enhance student learning (personal interview, November 18, 2018).

The Strategic Vision Advisory Council was composed of over 40 faculty and staff. "The early vision . . . was expressed and then distributed to this council for vigorous conversation. . . . We went through a series of iterations of the guiding document, based on the continued conversation within this very diverse advisory council . . . collectively we would come to agreement about the gaps or about slight changes in emphasis," said Co-Chair Ken Peterson, who is now dean of the faculty (personal interview, December 14, 2018). This iterative process generated considerable support and ensured the Furman Advantage was derived from institutional passions and strengths (K. Peterson, personal interview, December 14, 2018). The Furman Advantage was voted on and approved by the faculty in September of 2016.

Furman is 1 of the 4 institutions supported by the Duke Endowment, which provided significant funding to the initiative once it was approved. Furman received nearly $50 million from the endowment to support the Furman Advantage, both to launch the effort and to ensure its effective implementation and long-term success. Roughly half of that sum was invested in the university endowment in support of scholarship funds. Another $10 million went to the endowment in support of student experiences, $5 million was used to upgrade the campus technology systems, and a final $10 million was to be distributed in increments over a 5-year period to support the Furman Advantage (E. Davis, personal interview, November 18; 2018, Kovacs, 2016).

A Student-Centered Approach

The distinction of student-centric, as opposed to program-centric, is central to the Furman Advantage, and indeed to the distinctive program model. President Davis illustrated the distinction through the lens of Furman's May X experiences (short study away trips following the semester in May). One such trip to Rome was popular, but prior to the Furman Advantage only a small percentage of students could participate—only 17 of the 95 applicants in a given year, for example. Prior to the Furman Advantage, no one was asking about the 78 students who were not selected, and in the metric of programmatic success, it was indeed a successful, in-demand program. When the metric was shifted to measure success based on the student experience, the program needed to be evaluated with a different lens, as it was successfully serving only a minority of those interested (E. Davis, personal interview, November 18, 2018).

"If we're going to guarantee experiences for every student that connect their academics to experiences in the real world . . . research, internships, and other opportunities, we have to think on a student-by-student basis," said President Davis. "In that sense, we've transformed how we think about delivering a comprehensive education for our students" (personal interview, November 18, 2018).

Thinking from the student perspective requires the university to transcend the traditional organizational pillars of a college campus. Students do not tend to think about administration, staff, and faculty; they think about connections, experiences, and individuals. Integrating these aspects of the campus from a structural and learning perspective has been essential to the approach of the Furman Advantage (C. Carson, personal interview, December 14, 2018).

The collaboration across campus will continue past the building process. "The whole Furman Advantage plan requires that we on the academic side and our colleagues on the student life side see the world through a similar lens and that we're all working toward the same outcome," said Dean of the Faculty Ken Peterson. "The collaboration we have today between student life and academic affairs is, I think, exceptional and it has to remain that way for the Furman Advantage to fully materialize" (personal interview, December 14, 2018).

Data and Assessment

A central question of the Strategic Vision Advisory Council was defining what successful student outcomes would be. The result, according to Assistant Vice President for Assessment and Institutional Effectiveness David Eubanks, is a general structure of integration, reflection, and impact that is not overly prescriptive. This challenges the campus and the assessment process to "take each student seriously as an individual."

Furman is asking students if experiences were meaningful, and if so, how. One such effort asks students to provide an inventory of their experiences. From this list, students are asked what the most impactful experience was, and why. The goal is to allow the students to define their experience and build from that, rather than adhere too rigidly to a standardized approach. The answers are more complex, varied, and nuanced than what might result from the use of a standardized test (D. Eubanks, personal interview, December 14, 2018). The approach makes assessment more human and personal, using open-response questions when necessary and numbers when appropriate. Most importantly, it allows Furman to not only to capture the fact of an experience but also understand the value of that experience. Text analysis and other new statistical methods now allow the connection between qualitative and quantitative assessments (D. Eubanks, personal interview, December 14, 2018).

Associate Provost for Engaged Learning Beth Pontari, who oversees the effort to guarantee every student an impactful experience, is equally concerned with data collection. "My job is to somehow make sure I track every single student. . . . Once you are tracking them all then you can assess them well . . . [and] ensure that [the experiences are of] high quality" (personal interview, December 14, 2018). Success for Pontari is ensuring that 100% of students have a life-changing, impactful experience. The collection of this data will allow for what Pontari terms *surgical initiatives* to fill any gaps that are found. Such gaps could be transportation issues, financial barriers, or other life events not readily apparent without personalized assessment (B. Pontari, personal interview, December 14, 2018).

This understanding will stem from data collected at a multitude of points and from a variety of sources. Students answer a survey regarding beliefs and behaviors, including those about outcomes and experiences, at the end of each semester. Likewise, students complete an assessment before and after they conduct summer research or participate in a summer internship or study away program. Faculty also rate students on outcomes. Each faculty member fills out a brief questionnaire for each student, answering questions about, for instance, a student's writing ability. The questions and answers are brief, to keep the time commitment reasonable. While the data are not considered on an individual level due to the subjectivity of individual responses, on the whole they become rich (D. Eubanks, personal interview, December 14, 2018). The method allows for the collection of many more data points per year than the traditional methods of assessment. It provides enough data, said Eubanks, "to overcome the noisiness of the individuals and see the trends" (personal interview, December 14, 2018). Such data allow Furman to measure things like the efficacy of a trip to the writing lab on campus and can be aggregated across different campus populations (D. Eubanks, personal interview, December 14, 2018).

Faculty assessment has also shifted in concert with the Furman Advantage. While mentoring has always been a responsibility of faculty listed in the faculty handbook, it is now included in each faculty member's annual self-evaluation. Administered by the faculty status committee responsible for merit, tenure, and promotion, the section asks faculty to describe the ways in which they developed as an adviser and a mentor and what they did to support students in these roles (M. Horhota, personal interview, December 14, 2018).

Building on Strengths

Members of the Furman leadership team are quick to point out that the Furman Advantage builds on the strengths of Furman already in place. It builds on an assessment of "what Furman's capabilities are, what we really could be world-class at, and what we could do with those strengths and values to bridge the gap between higher ed and the value that parents and prospective students are looking for," said Ken Peterson (personal interview, December 14, 2018). Research, internships, and study away had existed at Furman for 40 years. The Furman Advantage "was built on the DNA of the institution," said Connie Carson (personal interview, December 14, 2018).

The building process involved creating several new administrative roles. Both the new associate provost for engaged learning and associate dean of mentoring and advising came from the existing faculty. New administrative positions were added in a strategic manner and have helped move the initiatives forward. They are designed to leverage strengths and add crucial support for professional development as the campus integrates the Furman Advantage into its practices and processes (B. Pontari, personal interview, December 14, 2018). These new administrative positions enhance the vision by both enabling Furman to get the outcomes desired with the Furman Advantage and ensuring that the burden of success is not placed directly on the backs of individual faculty (K. Peterson, personal interview, December 14, 2018).

Outcomes

There is reason to be optimistic that the undifferentiated regional college described in the 2015 Art & Science report is becoming more distinct. Furman has completed 2 enrollment cycles since the inception of the Furman Advantage. In building the differentiation that was so absent in the 2015 report, Furman has sought to tighten its focus on the traditional metrics of prestige for the private liberal arts college. Furman expects to report an admit rate of 57% for the fall 2019 cohort, down from the 68% rate reported in the 2016–2017 cycle (M. Hendricks, personal interview, March 29, 2019; U.S. Department of Education, 2017). Average test scores are similarly increasing (Furman is test-optional), and the discount rate has dropped (M. Hendricks, personal interview, March 29, 2019). As important to the institution is the rightsizing and retention of the class. Furman is not trying to grow its student body; if anything it expects to reduce it slightly as its student profile improves (M. Hendricks, personal interview, March 29, 2019). Furman's retention from first to second year has moved from 89% in 2015 to 93% in 2017 (U.S. Department of Education, 2017).

These shifts in enrollment metrics support Furman's qualitative assessment that it is on the right track. The value proposition that is the Furman Advantage can be offered more readily by Furman than by the large institutions like Clemson University and the University of South Carolina, with whom Furman routinely has cross-applications. The differentiation provided by the Furman Advantage serves as a vehicle for the institution's continued alignment with elite liberal arts institutions, its expected metrics, and the increased demand resultant from achieving those metrics. Thus, the quality of the student body itself, attracted in part to the value proposed by the Furman Advantage, will enhance the prestige and reputation of the institution and provide the differentiation Furman seeks (M. Hendricks, personal interview, March 29, 2018).

Conclusion

Coordination and consistency are key to the actualization of the Furman Advantage. Since the experience is a pathway that each student travels, success is contingent on students being exposed equally to pathway opportunities regardless of the variety of teachers and advisers with whom they will work. It is a delicate process, for the journey of each student need not be the same for a successful outcome. The Furman Advantage doesn't dictate the exact path a student will take; rather, it guarantees quality options along the way, and the guidance to explore them effectively. Each student will interact with the Furman Advantage differently; the reflection and mentoring through the process are what lead to the Furman Advantage.

The definition of *success* itself is part of that mission. The Furman Advantage rejects directly the notion that success is quantified only through graduation rates. Success in this vision is achieved when students experience a high level of well-being and engagement in college, and that experience translates into their postcollege endeavors. Students learn to reflect and articulate their experiences, first at Furman, and later into a narrative beneficial for employment and graduate school. "Part of the challenge for liberal arts colleges today is to avoid entirely the debate about whether it's career or not career," says Ken Peterson. "It's hard to live a purposeful life without a meaningful career, and we all want students to have a purposeful life, right?" (personal interview, December 14, 2018).

Figure 6.6. Furman University at a glance

Endowment	$703 million
Student-to-Faculty Ratio	10:1
Enrollment	2,949
Four-Year Graduation Rate	73%
Six-Year Graduation Rate	81%
Key Elements of the Curriculum	Distinctive student experience, the Furman Advantage 60 programs integrated and grounded in the liberal arts and sciences

Note: U.S. Department of Education (2017c).

7

UNDERSTANDING THE
EXPANSION MODEL

The fourth model for small colleges and universities is more clearly committed to growth, more market driven, and more explicitly developed as a business model based primarily on enrollment metrics. This is the expansion model. The expansion model responds to market trends, often with some alacrity. The main institutional focus is enrollment growth, and campuses evaluate and develop academic programs with a strong consideration for existing and potential student demand, as well as the needs of the local community.

There are three ways in which campuses in the expansion model attempt to increase student enrollment: by adding new programs or growing existing high-demand programs, by adding new locations, and by adding different methods of program delivery. The range of programs can vary widely at these institutions, depending on location, institutional strengths, and capacity. For example, a campus with an existing health sciences core may expand enrollment in programs such as nursing, while adding new programs in areas such as occupational therapy or pharmacy. If there is sufficient market, addition may also be pursued in areas that are not aligned with current programs but have proven demand, such as computer science or business analytics. Growth may also be concentrated more in graduate programs, where high demand and low tuition discounting can add significant revenue to the operating budget.

Along with growth in high-demand programs, institutions in the expansion model often add new off-campus sites in areas that are believed to be underserved for higher education. Off-campus sites are often targeted in their programming and typically focus on regional market needs or specific programs and courses that are not expensive to deliver but fill a market void.

Different program delivery modalities, including online, limited residency, and hybrid programs, are another way in which expansion model campuses add enrollment. Hybrid and online models are increasingly important in offering degrees for adults and working professionals and may become the dominant form of program delivery in areas that are particularly attractive to working adults, such as graduate business offerings or undergraduate degree completion programs. They are also a strong element in many certificate programs and in helping working adults retool for targeted business needs.

The capital priorities of the expansion model campus reflect the shift or growth in educational programs. New or renovated campus facilities are created to support the new programs. These campuses often see the addition of facilities for the health sciences or computing, facilities that may replace, or at least overshadow, the old spaces dedicated to, for example, the visual and performing arts. They may also purchase, rent, or build new off-site facilities that are situated more directly in a program's service area, such as dedicated off-site programs in education or the health sciences. Rapidly adding new programs can place stress on infrastructure but promises new revenue streams in return. Over time, the result is often a shift in educational focus through accreted responses to shifting student demand.

This response to market demand may have a concomitant effect on enrollment in traditional programs, while the proportion of students in the liberal arts may become a smaller percentage of the student population. Unlike the traditional or the integrated model, the expansion model does not necessarily retain a strong fealty to the liberal arts. Unlike the distinctive program model, it does not attempt to create a common educational experience beyond general education requirements. By committing to market responsiveness they are often more data-driven, and more nimble, than most colleges and universities.

Defining Features of the Expansion Model

Many institutions in the expansion model began as more traditional liberal arts institutions. As they sought additional enrollment, many also had a period more closely defined by the integrated model. They may retain a college or some programs focused on the liberal arts, but after multiple years of program additions (and perhaps closures in less well-enrolled areas), their overall educational model is less concerned with integration. Enrollment growth has likely led to a more disaggregated set of academic offerings, more akin to a loose confederacy than an integrated model.

Because the expansion model is based on market demand, student recruitment is driven by program and may highlight individual programs more than the institution as a whole; the attractiveness and student demand for programs tend to define the campus to prospective students. In recent years, for many campuses in this model, this has meant a focus on programs in the health sciences, business, film and media, or technology fields. It has also meant an increase in online and hybrid educational delivery models.

The expansion model is driven by a business mind-set, with a focus on return on investment. Thus, campuses committed to expansion evaluate both market and cost and allocate resources accordingly. While there may be a strong market for programs in the data sciences or nursing, for example, such programs often require significant physical infrastructure, discrete accreditation and the concomitant staff support, and specialized faculty expertise. These factors will be carefully evaluated before the campus commits to adding new initiatives.

Similarly, expanding into the hybrid or online mode of delivery may yield an increase in students, but expansion also requires strong learning management systems and a different type of pedagogical expertise than that asked of faculty in the classroom. A full evaluation of the cost of faculty and program development and delivery, as well as market demand, guides the decision about where to invest and, ultimately, to expand.

Adding new physical delivery sites is another area that needs thorough analysis in this model. A new site usually requires investment before the fiscal return is realized, whether the site is purchased or leased. Before a new program is added, robust market analysis will include not only the likely student demand and cost of the program but also the length of time and amount of investment required before the program yields financial returns to the institution.

Integrating, consolidating, or closing programs requires a similar analysis. While some of the more traditional programs may not have significant market demand, in many cases they are also relatively inexpensive to deliver, as they do not require specialized equipment, programmatic accreditation, or new infrastructure.

Students in the expansion model will include both traditional college students and a number of nontraditional-age students, attracted by the flexibility of hybrid, online, and site-based courses. Working adults and those returning to complete their degrees usually find the greater flexibility of these courses more responsive to their needs, as they are frequently managing significant work and family responsibilities. Further, adult students are not seeking the same type of college experience as traditional-age students and are usually more clear and specific in their reasons for undertaking higher education.

Institutions in the expansion model retain a central campus as the core of educational and administrative activity, even as they may have a number of programs at additional sites. They often have a larger nonresident and commuter student population, reflecting the range of programs and delivery options they provide.

Expansion model institutions are nimble and data driven. To succeed in providing high-demand programs, they must identify and capture new markets before the market is saturated. This requires them to work closely with their communities to understand business and civic needs, as well as to assess the demand for specific degrees and credentials. They often have a sophisticated process for analyzing the cost, time to launch, and expected return on investment for new programs.

Inherent Strengths of the Expansion Model

The expansion model is clear in its purpose and its progress can be quantitatively evaluated. Growth in enrollment and in net tuition revenue is the goal, and by using that measure the campus can align behind very clear targets and expend energy on market analysis and cost of program delivery. It takes discipline and focus to implement this approach, but the return can be readily measured.

One of the strengths of the expansion model is its responsiveness to regional needs or the career aspirations of students. By adding new programs that fit a niche within a region, or that respond to growing interest in particular credentials, the expansion model can effectively build enrollment and serve students. Appropriate planning can ensure that new programs are created that meet standards for academic quality, while market surveys can gauge the likely attraction of new programs.

When built from institutional strength, new programs can reinforce an institution's status and identity. This is particularly true when new programs align with long-standing campus mission and ethos; for example, adding programs in nursing, occupational therapy, and other health professions has been a natural fit for many campuses with a mission of service. Campuses with strong economics, business, or technology programs can often elevate their position by developing new offerings in, for example, cybersecurity or data analytics.

The growth and innovation required in the expansion model can reinforce creativity and reward the most dynamic and committed faculty and staff. Knowing that they can build a program that derives from their strengths and expands their expertise and offerings is an energizing experience, one that can lead to a healthy climate of innovation for the institution. Depending on the campus and its mission and vision, these programs can provide internal cross-subsidies for legacy programs, although sometimes they simply replace those programs.

Inherent Challenges of the Expansion Model

The challenges in the expansion model are more significant than may first appear. The business and market-driven mind-set that is at the core of this model is in tension with many basic tenets of academe. The expansion model needs nimbleness, while securing accreditation and other accepted measures of quality takes time. For example, to hire well-qualified faculty, the campus likely needs to offer tenure or some form of long-term job security. But that same job security commits the program to specific faculty skills and can make it difficult for the institution to continue to adapt.

Adding programs with quality also requires a significant up-front investment in infrastructure—along with qualified faculty, most new programs need additional investments in physical space, specialized equipment, program design, and marketing. If it is a hybrid or an online program, both technology infrastructure and professional development are essential. These investments are greater if the new program is not in an area of strength for the campus—for example, starting a nursing program without an existing solid core of programs in the health sciences or creating cybersecurity programs without substantial existing quantitative or computer science expertise. This investment must occur before the programs are launched. Such capacity challenges limit the ability of some campuses to expand at all and limit the speed with which new efforts can be launched. They also highlight the need for due diligence in identifying new programs that will be successful for the long-term.

The expansion model is dependent on market research being not only accurate but also predictive for an extended period. But the market is not stable. There are numerous cases around the country of programs that were once major drivers of enrollment and revenue for institutions (e.g., law schools) that have now become a burden. Because the campus has already invested in the faculty and infrastructure necessary to produce such programs, it is very difficult to discontinue them if the market changes.

Further, if the expansion model is explicitly designed to build a budget on year-over-year enrollment growth, it will eventually challenge one of the core strengths of the small independent college or university: an intimate setting and small classes with individualized attention to students. Thus, while the expansion model has the potential to support flagging enrollment and realize additional revenue for some campuses, it can also challenge the core mission and long-term sustainability of an institution. And it is a difficult model to implement in a short time frame.

Many campuses that have moved from the traditional or integrated model to the expansion model find that the role of the liberal arts is unclear or contested. This can pose both a philosophical and a practical challenge. Philosophically, it raises fundamental questions about institutional mission and about educational coherence. Practically, legacy programs may also have a large number of tenured faculty, with the contractual and ethical obligations inherent in that relationship.

Contemporary Examples of the Expansion Model

Two institutions representing the expansion model are Chapman University and Utica College. They have contrasting histories and have taken different approaches to expansion but have each employed specific aspects of the expansion model to make fundamental changes to their institutions. Chapman is self-described as being "run with a business mind-set," while Utica explains that it is "aggressively entrepreneurial."

Chapman, in Southern California, was once a small, traditional, faith-based college. The institution has focused on market-driven program addition, primarily (but not exclusively) in a campus-based format. From a largely traditional undergraduate college, Chapman used aggressive enrollment targets to grow dramatically over the course of several decades. Today, the university houses a school of business and economics; a college of educational studies; a college of film and media arts; a college of health and behavioral sciences; a school of law; a college of performing arts; a school of pharmacy; and a college of science and technology and traditional college of arts, humanities, and social sciences.

Utica, in upstate New York, is another example of the expansion model from a very different history and geographic position. In recent years, Utica has explicitly expanded programs in high-demand areas, particularly the health sciences. In order to reach a market beyond its upstate New York population, Utica has also actively expanded its online programming, resulting in significant enrollment growth beyond the core campus. Campus leadership works closely with faculty to create new programs built on existing educational strengths.

Utica also used its entrepreneurial approach to market analysis to implement a tuition reset. This process has served the institution well, something that is not always the case with such moves—and a testament to its considered and data-driven approach.

Both Chapman and Utica have built strong ties to their region and used those connections to help assess the value of additional programs. For example, Chapman's location in Orange County, California, inspired the creation of a college of film and media arts. Utica's location in a more economically distressed region of the country led to a strong commitment to health sciences, programs that reliably lead to postgraduation employment.

Each institution has developed a clear, thoughtful, data-driven process for evaluating the potential of new programs and new delivery methods. Utica used its early adopter status in online education to expand its offerings in that area, while Chapman recently added a new site in Irvine, California, based on a thorough assessment of regional needs.

While these two campuses are very different in profile and history, their success in implementing the expansion model—amid enrollment downturns for many colleges and universities—is valuable and instructive.

PROFILE OF AN EXPANSION MODEL INSTITUTION: CHAPMAN UNIVERSITY

Field research and draft compilation of this campus profile conducted by Jaime Morgen while an EdM student at the Harvard Graduate School of Education

Driving through Chapman's campus in Orange County, California feels almost like taking a journey through time. What started as a smaller, regionally focused, private college has transformed into an institution that is now much larger, with more diverse programming and reach than a few decades ago. Originally called Hesperian College, the institution was founded in 1861 by members of the Disciples of Christ. Even at its beginning, Chapman was fulfilling a need for members of the local community, as a public school system did not yet exist in the state of California. Founded as a religious school, Chapman has always opened its doors to both men and women, as well as members of all races, believing that higher education could be for every one. At the turn of the twentieth century, Chapman worked to develop its institutional identity in a growing higher education landscape. By 1935, the institution was officially renamed Chapman College (after primary benefactor and trustee C.C. Chapman) and in 1954, Chapman College acquired the land that would become its campus in Orange County. Years later, in

1991, Chapman College became Chapman University, and the growth has not stopped since (Chapman, n.d.b).

More than 15 years ago, in the 2003–2004 school year, the university included 8 different schools (the George L. Argyros School of Business and Economics, the school of communication arts, the school of education, the Lawrence and Kristina Dodge College of Film and Media, the school of law, the school of music, the Wilkinson College of Letters and Sciences, and Chapman University College for adult learners). There were approximately 5,000 full-time undergraduate and graduate students on its Orange County campus.

Since then, the size of the student body has grown considerably, and Chapman currently enrolls 8,542 students, including 6,410 undergraduates and 2,132 graduate students; 20% of students identify as first generation, while 40% identify as Persons of Color (POC). Students hail from 49 states, 2 territories, and 82 countries. Furthermore, the university has expanded its academic reach to include 11 different schools (the Wilkinson College of Arts, Humanities, and Social Sciences; the Argyros School of Business and Economics; the school of communication; the Donna Ford Attallah College of Educational Studies; the Fowler School of Engineering; the Dodge College of Film and Media Arts; the Crean College of Health and Behavioral Sciences; and the Fowler School of Law) and 110 areas of study. Students can pursue 1 of 123 undergraduate degrees and programs or 1 of 70 graduate degrees and programs.

President Daniele Struppa assumed office in 2016, after serving as provost and then chancellor at the university for 10 years. Struppa has adopted the strategy and built on the work of the previous president, James Doti, who was in office for a quarter of a century. Under Doti's presidency, the university established a pattern of assessing the needs of Orange County in terms of schools and programs, financially targeting a specific need at a time, and then moving on to the next program on the list. To continue the work of President Doti, President Struppa and the rest of the leadership team rely on highly specific strategic plans that are broken down into 5-year increments. President Struppa calls each strategic plan a "road map" consisting of goals, associated metrics, and required funding (D. Struppa, personal interview, November 21, 2018). When devising strategic plans, Struppa and his team rely on quantitative information, like survey results from students, faculty, and other members of the community. Harold Hewitt, executive vice president and chief operating officer, notes, "Each year I know what programs we are going to be adding, what sources of funding we targeted, and what triggers said we could move forward. Chapman's strategic plan is a big deal and is taken seriously" (personal interview, December 13, 2018). Hewitt says that the leadership and the board attempt to identify what will be successful in their own backyard (personal interview, December 13, 2018). For example, the Fowler School of Law is the first in the Orange County area, and the school of pharmacy is the first to be accredited in the surrounding area.

When Struppa began his tenure as president, he continued the process of identifying a specific niche and then establishing a new program. Struppa hired economist Vernon Smith to build an economics institute with a niche focus on experimental economics. Because very few other institutions are focusing on this specific area of economics, the program has attained status in its niche, not locally but only also in the national and international market.

Similarly, the Dodge College of Film and Media Arts (established in 1996 under President Doti's leadership) created a unique curriculum and draws students partially because of that curricular structure. While other programs require two years of general education before beginning film courses, the Dodge College's curriculum is more integrated and allows students to pick up a camera on their first day. The general education requirements are then distributed over the course of the undergraduate experience.

Strategic Planning Leads to Diversification

The most recently completed strategic plan—in effect from 2013 to 2018—revolved around moving into the health sciences and specifically focused on growing those programs, as well as establishing a school of pharmacy, and strengthening the university's commitment to undergraduate students. The prior 2008 to 2013 strategic plan was titled "A Path to National Stature." In those five years, the leadership team at Chapman focused on recruiting faculty with both national and international visibility, establishing various centers (e.g., the Economic Science Institute; the Institute for Quantum Studies; and the Institute for the Study of Religion, Economics, and Society) and expanding programs in the sciences (Chapman University, n.d.c). It is these detailed strategic plans that guided Chapman's implementing of new programs and qualitatively and quantitatively measured their progress.

The current strategic plan, which spans the 2018 to 2022 academic years, is named "Engineering the Future." The first, and largest, aspect of the current strategic plan is the establishment of the Fowler School of Engineering, which is slated to open in 2020. Recognizing that engineering undergraduate students have high earning potential, and also noticing that universities in the area struggled to produce the types of engineers that employers were seeking, leadership at Chapman decided that establishing a school of engineering would fill a need in the market.

Second, in the current strategic plan, Chapman is also focusing on expanding its research agenda. The goal is to enhance status and give students the tools to integrate their knowledge in both the laboratory and the classroom by supporting faculty development, expanding sponsored research, and increasing research technology. The current strategic plan also focuses on optimizing the campus footprint (including building dormitories to house 50% of the undergraduate population) and launching a comprehensive fundraising campaign (Chapman University, n.d.a).

The last part of the current strategic plan is the complete revamping of the Chapman experience. The manner in which the university has begun to make decisions in this area illustrates the unusual nature of Chapman's approach and highlights the institution's commitment to respond in a business-like manner to market pressures. Struppa describes the Chapman experience as all interactions with the university for current and future stakeholders. Rather than using a higher education research firm to evaluate current perceptions of Chapman, Struppa sought assistance from an iconic, if nonacademic, Chapman neighbor: the Disney Company. Struppa noted that Disney's brand loyalty and the experience the company creates is unparalleled, largely due to the emotional connection between the consumers and their experience. Chapman hired the Disney Institute to look at all processes on campus—from applying for admission, to calling the president's office, to visiting campus—and make recommendations to improve the customer experience.

In beginning its collaboration with the Disney Institute in 2017, Chapman characteristically relied on survey results to guide its work. The first step was to distribute a survey that allowed the institute to do a pulse check on the current campus climate. The survey yielded 2,450 responses from both internal and external stakeholders including undergraduate and graduate students, faculty, staff, administration, trustees, parents, and alumni. Using the data, the Disney Institute established three key areas that can be improved: employee care and recognition, leadership behavior, and communications. The hope is that through partnering with the Disney Institute, Chapman will become a place that "people fight to get into, don't want to leave, love to support, and never forget" (Chapman University, n.d.a).

Outcomes

It is evident from prior strategic plans that one of Chapman's consistent goals has been to increase undergraduate and graduate enrollment while simultaneously maintaining the quality of the student body. The student body has unequivocally grown: When Executive Vice President of University Advancement Sheryl Bourgeois first arrived at Chapman in 1998, the entire student body was around 1,300 students. In 2019, Chapman *graduated* over 1,700 students. Bourgeois notes, "What's also been unique, and somewhat unparalleled, is the fact that the university grew enrollment, student selectivity, and academic strength all while changing its physical plant" (personal interview, December 13, 2018). To account for this increase in enrollment, leadership at Chapman credits the addition of schools as well as the decision to go from a Division II athletic program to a Division III program. While some may think this decision is insignificant, it allowed the university to reinvest money that was being used for athletic scholarships and put it toward academic scholarships.

In addition to adding different colleges to the fabric of the university, Chapman has also widened its geographic reach. According to the current strategic plan, Chapman was primarily a southern California university in the year 2000, with 46% of the incoming class coming from the surrounding area. Almost 20 years later, by the fall of 2017, 17% of students came from the surrounding Orange County area (Chapman University, n.d.a).

As a response to increasing enrollment, a changing student body, and different outcome expectations, the university has undergone curricular reforms. Executive Vice President Bourgeois notes that even though the university is divided into different schools, every student is required to have a minor or cluster outside of their major. In this way, students have interdisciplinary studies built into their undergraduate education. Furthermore, new programs have been developed that are specifically designed to bring contrasting, but complementing, disciplines together. An example of such an interdisciplinary program is the new Smith Institute for Political Economy and Philosophy, which serves as a point of intersection for the study of humanities and economics. The institute was created in tandem by an economics professor and an English professor and is now made up of faculty from several different departments. The institute challenges students to reexamine seminal texts through an economics lens. Chapman is now developing a music business degree so students who specialize in music can start their own company or produce their own show. Executive Vice President Bourgeois comments, "We are blessed that our deans are open to collaboration" (personal interview, December 13, 2018).

Chapman has also looked to the greater Orange County community to support growth. The university recently purchased 25 acres of land in Irvine (less than 20 miles away from the main campus) to grow its health sciences graduate programs. By focusing on areas like physician's assistant studies, physical therapy, speech-language pathology, and pharmacy, Chapman is responding to market demand, as noted by Executive Vice President Bourgeois:

> Programs like PA [physician assistant] and pharmacy are less costly than a medical degree and the salaries are strong. For first-gen students, they can get working quicker and their debt load is significantly less. It ticks all the boxes— it addresses the changing demographics in high school students, it provides immediate opportunities for workforce development, and it is needed right now in Orange County. (personal interview, December 13, 2018)

This new physical space in Irvine will allow established programs to grow in size, and also allow the school to add more specialties (e.g., gerontology, audiology, and occupational therapy) as well as combined or accelerated bachelor's and master's degree programs. The leadership at Chapman is in agreement that this area—graduate programs in health-related fields that align with the needs of community—is where the next stage of institutional growth is likely to be.

Culture and Process

Chapman is run with a business mind-set, including specific, detailed, and data-driven processes for evaluating progress and problems. As we have seen, concurrent five-year strategic plans are detailed, assessed, and implemented. The university has remained transparent about its strategic plans; on the university website, one can access every previous strategic plan. In addition to reading about the goals that the university has in place, one can also dive into the specific metrics to see how goals are measured, and if they have been achieved.

Behind drastic shifts in student enrollment, increased academic offerings for undergraduate and graduate students, and curricular reform is a complete shift in the culture of the institution. President Struppa calls this cultural approach transformative. In fact, Struppa says, "In a way I think the cultural transformation has to be the first step" (personal interview, November 21, 2018).

With the changes going on at the university, it is not surprising that leadership has faced some resistance from some faculty members, especially in the liberal arts disciplines. Executive Vice President Bourgeois acknowledged this challenge and the reasons for it. "Let's face it," she said, "if there is any area that is going to be attacked for return on investment, it is some of the humanities . . . It's too bad for the academy" (personal interview, December 13, 2018).

Conclusion

Although Chapman was founded as a small religious college with a regional focus, its transformation has followed the expansion model. It is fully market driven, and has focused on expanding its offerings, footprint, and programs based on data analysis and market demands. The new strategic plan and the new campus in Irvine continue this trajectory. President Struppa wants to elevate the university to the point where it becomes an integral part of the Orange County area. President Struppa comments,

> I asked myself, 'If tomorrow morning, the board of trustees were to decide to move Chapman to Nevada, would anybody care? Would anyone start a petition to keep us here?' The goal for the university is to be so crucial to the community that if we decide to move away, we would want the mayor to say 'no, don't go away.' I would want everyone to come up and say 'Chapman is too important to us.' (personal interview, November 21, 2019)

Figure 7.1. Chapman University at a glance.

Endowment	$301.5 million
Student-to-Faculty Ratio	14:1
Enrollment	8,542
Four-Year Graduation Rate	69%
Six-Year Graduation Rate	79%
Key Elements of the Curriculum	Nearly 200 areas of study split across 11 different schools

Note: Chapman University (2016).

PROFILE OF AN EXPANSION MODEL
INSTITUTION: UTICA COLLEGE

Field research and draft compilation of this campus profile conducted by Carlos Benjamin Castellon while an EdM student at the Harvard Graduate School of Education

Utica College is located in central New York State in the county of Oneida. Utica's origins are tied to Syracuse University. In 1930, Syracuse began offering extension courses through a separate branch campus in the Utica, New York area. After recognizing the impact this separate branch campus was having, along with growing support from community leaders in the city of Utica, Syracuse University officially established and launched Utica College in 1946. The new institution was originally located in the downtown area known as Oneida Square but moved in 1961 to the current site off Burrstone Road. Utica College became both financially and legally independent from Syracuse University in 1995 and began offering master's and doctoral degrees in 1998. The college eventually transitioned into the final stages of independence in 2008, when it began to offer its own undergraduate degree programs (Utica College, n.d.a).

As a private institution of higher education, Utica College aims to offer students a comprehensive academic experience. As of 2019, Utica College has a 13:1 student-to-faculty ratio, reflecting its small college roots. There are more than 5,000 students ranging from traditional 4-year students to transfer students, graduate students, and international students. In 2017, 67% of the Utica College student population were White, 11.5% were Black or African American, 3.5% were Asian, 9.3% were Hispanic or Latino, and 2.5% identified as 2 or more races (U.S. Department of Education, 2017e).

The mission of Utica College is to impact the world and society through its students, and the college's goal is to be the nation's most innovative small university, one that inspires students to create a future beyond their imagining (Utica College, n.d.a). This mission and ambition are illustrated more fully through the Utica College mission statement:

> Utica College educates students for rewarding careers, responsible citizenship, enlightened leadership, and fulfilling lives by integrating liberal and professional study, by creating a community of learners with diverse experiences and perspectives, by balancing a commitment to its local heritage with global outreach, by encouraging lifelong learning, and by promoting scholarship in the belief that the discovery and application of knowledge enrich teaching, learning, and society. (Utica College Mission Statement, n.d.b)

This mission statement aligns with the Utica College values that include individual attention to students; lifelong learning; community and professional service; diversity of perspective, background, and experience in an increasingly global society; ethical behavior and integrity in all that is done; pragmatic approaches to teaching and learning; continual improvement in educational and operational quality; freedom of expression and the open sharing of ideas and creativity; open, honest, and collegial communication; and the well-being of others (Utica College, n.d.a).

Academics and Program Structure

Although a relatively small, private institution, Utica College offers a wide range of programs. Utica College's academic offerings include over 40 undergraduate programs, 36 minors, 20 graduate programs, and several graduate certificates. Of the undergraduate programs, the most popular bachelor's degree programs are both in the health sciences: registered nursing and general health services (Data USA, 2019). Utica College emphasizes experiential learning and research both inside and outside of the classroom via educational opportunities such as study abroad, community caring, and on-site research facilities.

Many of the graduate programs and certificates are also offered online. These online programs cover a wide range of disciplines, including several in the health sciences, cybersecurity, economics, criminology, and business administration. Additionally, Utica College also has a strong partnership with Mohawk Valley Community College, including specialized transfer agreements focused on Utica College's construction management and cybersecurity programs.

Adopting the Expansion Model: Two Key Initiatives

In evaluating the changing higher education landscape and emerging challenges such as decreases in enrollment and a flattening of net revenue, Utica College adopted an aggressively entrepreneurial response. Many campus officials stated that Utica College had to adopt a unique and aggressive approach to respond to the challenges facing the institution. According to these officials, the two main areas that have been employed are the development of new academic programming and a tuition reset. These two avenues are Utica College's proactive response to the challenges that small, independent colleges are facing and the areas in which the college hopes to continue to build upon for sustained growth.

Utica College has added new programs by increasing its offerings in distance learning. This strategy builds on an existing strength, as Utica College was an early adopter in online education. Dating back to the late 1990s, there was a focus placed upon online education that has since grown and become nationally recognized. The early and sustained concentration of online education provided the infrastructure and expertise for Utica College to introduce several new online graduate degrees in recent years, including an online doctoral program in physical therapy. In addition, the college launched both an online degree program for moving from a registered nurse certification to a Bachelor of Science in Nursing and an accelerated Bachelor of Science in Nursing. Most recently, the college launched an online Master of Science in Nursing.

Initially, most of Utica College's online programs focused on the graduate market, while undergraduate offerings were more traditionally residential. Extensive market research also showed a demand for targeted online undergraduate degrees, and Utica College sought to use its existing success in online education to create undergraduate online degrees. As Jeffrey Gates, senior vice president for student life and enrollment management, stated,

> There was a need to take what was happening with our online graduate education and introduce it to our undergraduate students. Our RN-to-BSN program has been successful both for the students enrolled as well as a means for Utica College to diversify our revenue. (personal interview, February 8, 2019)

Associate Vice President of Information Technology and Institutional Research Matthew Carr reinforced the importance of online programming to the larger institutional strategy, saying, "I think where we've seen opportunities to keep growing over time is in our expansion of online learning as well as looking at market niche opportunities in other states and other areas" (personal interview, February 8, 2019).

Another way that Utica College approached the challenges of small colleges was through newly formed partnerships with Wiley Education Services and Orbis Education. In conjunction with Orbis Education, Utica College developed an accelerated Bachelor of Science in Nursing program in two locations (New York and Florida) that features an online curriculum, onsite instruction, and clinical rotations (Utica College, n.d.a). The Wiley Education Services and College partnership dates back to 2004 and recently grew to provide more services and support in the areas of recruitment, enrollment, and retention services and strategies. President Laura Casamento spoke about the relationship and importance of working with partners, saying, "These partnerships with Wiley Education Services and with Orbis Education created the opportunity for new market programming. I keep in close contact with my counterpart at our partners for successful collaboration" (personal interview, February 8, 2019).

Utica College also used an entirely different, nonprogrammatic strategy to reposition itself in the market and address the changes in higher education through a comprehensive tuition reset. The tuition reset was developed in response to a flattening of net tuition revenue. This initiative started as a two-year research project that projected an unsustainable tuition and aid model in the existing form. While tuition increases were being applied annually at Utica College, the college found itself making less in net revenue due to the discount rate—the amount of aid necessary to compete for, recruit, and enroll undergraduate students. Additionally, the sticker price itself appeared to be a barrier to Utica College for some students and their families.

Matthew Carr, associate vice president of information technology and institutional research, spoke about this process more, stating that

> When we decided to reset our tuition, we opened our opportunities up for students and families that may not have considered us in the past, [but who] actually have the means to pay for Utica College. What we saw was both an increase in enrollment, and an increase in the net tuition revenue as well, allowing us to be more sustainable. (personal interview, February 8, 2019)

President Laura Casamento played an active role in the development and design of the tuition reset; she was executive vice president and chief advancement officer through its creation and now oversees its ongoing implementation as president. She stated, "Being a tuition-dependent school, we had to look at this specific avenue and be as transparent as possible in trying to strengthen the undergraduate revenue stream" (L. Casamento, personal interview, February 8, 2019).

Process

The process Utica College undertook to implement these changes was comprehensive and thorough. Regarding the tuition reset, the institution underwent an intensive internal process to evaluate potential gains and risks of what would be a significant change to the financial model. In addition, Utica College partnered with Ruffalo Noel Levitz, an enrollment management consulting firm, to conduct a market analysis and identify areas of particular challenge within the college. Campus administrators presented the resultant tuition reset plan to a small working group of trustees, which was then presented to the entire board of trustees for final authorization.

Faculty were integral to developing, evaluating, and supporting implementation of these changes at Utica College. Matthew Carr spoke about the entrepreneurial role of faculty in bringing ideas to the forefront, stating,

> "But that, like I said, comes from our faculty. While some of that was happening under our former president and continues to happen under President Casamento, we have a very innovative faculty who are looking for those opportunities and who are really attuned to the marketplace" (M. Carr, personal interview, February 8, 2019).

President Casamento further expanded on the role of faculty and the relationship they have with administration and stated, "Even if we think there is something bubbling up in the market, we'll bring ideas to the faculty and see if we can run with it or not, because if we do not have faculty championing something, then it's just not going to happen" (L. Casamento, personal interview, February 8, 2019).

Outcomes

To date, the 2016 tuition reset has had several positive outcomes. First, the transparency about cost and the lower sticker price led to an increase in applications and subsequently enrollment. Second, returning students at Utica College began to realize savings, as well as a decrease in the overall student loan debt. Third, the college was able to serve more students from different backgrounds, particularly new students from families with incomes less than $100,000. Finally, Utica College was able to increase net tuition revenue per undergraduate, moving from $13,906 in 2015–2016 to $15,610 in 2017–2018 (Utica College, n.d.a).

Conclusion

In response to the growing changes in higher education, Utica College has adopted an explicitly entrepreneurial approach. Indeed, President Casamento stated that "if we're able to find that program where we are good at it and we can compete and then we say let's make sure we can resource it properly and that the numbers work, then let's go. . . . It's not enough for Utica College to go year-to-year and be sustainable. We've got to set the course so that this institution is here for the next hundred years. It's making our foundation so strong that we set the path for the future" (personal interview, February 2, 2019).

Through President Casamento's leadership and committed engagement from administration and faculty, Utica College has begun to see results of its innovative strategy. The tuition reset and expanded partnerships via academic programming created a diversification of revenue streams that the administration emphasized as instrumental areas of growth and sustainability.

Figure 7.2. Utica College at a glance.

Endowment	$25.8 million
Student Faculty Ratio	13:1
Enrollment	5,258
Four-Year Graduation Rate	42%
Six-Year Graduation Rate	54%
Key Elements of the Curriculum	48 majors Blend of liberal arts and professional education Postbaccalaureate certificates Master's degree Doctoral degree—professional practice Online graduate courses Accelerated Bachelor Degree in Nursing

Note: U.S. Department of Education (2017e).

8

UNDERSTANDING
THE DISTRIBUTED
UNIVERSITY MODEL

Finally the fifth model for small colleges and universities is the distributed university model. The distributed university model receives its name because its educational offerings are distributed over a large geographic region, across numerous programs and disciplines, and through a variety of educational delivery systems.

As educational technology has become more sophisticate and as student demographics, employment demands, and cost pressures have shifted, some colleges have made dramatic adjustments to respond to the changing market. The distributed model extends the strategy of the expansion model by aggressively adding high-demand programs (both degree and nondegree), expanding to multiple sites, and using an array of educational delivery systems with an emphasis in online and limited residency learning.

The distributed university seeks new markets that often operate separately from the original core undergraduate education delivered at a single, campus-based site. Depending on the level of growth, branch campuses and online programs may come to define the institution, while the old undergraduate residential program operates somewhat independently or even ceases to exist. The overall approach is nimble, employs a high degree of technology-enabled courses and programs, and is driven by enrollment and market trends. Heavy investment in technology, data analysis, marketing, and customer service are hallmarks of the distributed model.

The advent of the distributed model can be traced to the growth in employment-driven programs, the demand for more skill-based education, expansion of adult degree completion programs, and the increasing sophistication of educational technology. At the end of the last century, many small colleges began to offer more off-campus courses and programs designed to boost enrollment and meet the needs of the job market. A number of small colleges developed online and hybrid courses to supplement their on-campus offerings. Over time, many small colleges also developed certificate programs and summer immersion programs to generate revenue, fully utilize facilities, and extend the academic calendar. The distributed model builds on these changes and often leverages them to extend the reach of the campus and to use technology to serve a broader range of students. The distributed institution reaches beyond a single, site-based campus, adding programs and sites where there is a demonstrated demand, often in partnership with schools, governments, or businesses.

These changes often lead to a strategic focus on career preparation and training and to the campus having greater appeal for nontraditional-age students. Programs offered in this model are aligned with employment trends and may be designed to provide workforce training for a specific industry. This workforce focus means there may be a substantial set of credential and certificate offerings as well as degree programs.

Aggressive use of educational technology has also sometimes led to changes in the academic calendar. Distributed campuses may move more toward a cohort-based model or move students through courses at a more accelerated speed than the usual degree program. Some institutions have adopted competency-based education, which focuses on skill development and allows for asynchronous student movement toward a degree. The focus is on responding to student timelines and interest, increased flexibility, and adapting with speed to changes in the market.

It is important to note that institutions that successfully adopt the distributed model are, almost by definition, no longer small colleges or universities. They may remain private institutions, but this model depends on economies of scale for its financial success; in addition, it is largely nonresidential and appeals mostly to adult students. Thus, any small college or university deciding to adopt this approach is, fundamentally, deciding to change at least part of its identity. It can, however, be a viable path forward, especially for institutions in regions that are losing large numbers of traditional-age students or for campuses that are already experienced in developing quality online and hybrid programs. These programs can even subsidize a traditional core campus.

Defining Features of the Distributed University Model

There are five defining features of the distributed model. Some are common to other models, but only the distributed university implements all of these approaches.

The first defining feature is that campuses that have adopted the distributed university model have multiple sites for program delivery. The sites not located on the original campus are designed to either provide a particular program to a specific region or operate as branch campuses, with multiple programs offered out of an extended site. The most common programs offered through such sites align with government needs or business demands—programs such as accounting, criminal justice, cybersecurity, or teacher education. In addition, sites beyond the main campus that serve as satellites or branch campuses are usually reaching a region, or a student population, that is underserved for higher education. These branch campuses may not offer the full range of courses offered on the main campus but rather serve as regional education centers. For example, St. Leo University has developed nearly 40 education centers throughout the country that are focused on meeting the needs of specific locations. The university also offers a significant number of online courses, all while maintaining a strong central campus grounded in the liberal arts. Webster University, based in St. Louis, has built an integrated global network of campuses; some are traditional and some are specifically designed for working adults.

The second defining feature of the distributed university is the range of programs it offers. Programs are focused on market and may include degree and nondegree offerings. Programs are offered at the undergraduate and graduate level, and often graduate degree programs extend to the doctoral level. They also offer a substantial number of certificates and other credentials designed to support student professional development and advancement.

Third, campuses in the distributed model actively utilize technology to deliver courses and programs, as well as manage customer service. They offer a mix of online, hybrid, limited residency, and site-based programs, usually as a way to dramatically expand their market.

Fourth, distributed model institutions may forego the usual academic calendar and evaluation process. They offer support services through technology and provide asynchronous individualized learning options or options to learn in small cohorts that begin whenever a sufficient cadre of students is ready to start the program. The most sophisticated may use competency-based education to evaluate students' learning outcomes, and often these evaluations are fully online.

Fifth and finally, the distributed model focuses on providing education at a much lower cost than the usual high-tuition, high-financial-aid approach used by most small colleges. Campuses in this space are focused on economies of scale, and their reach allows them to operate in a much different financial manner than the typical small college. Indeed, as we will see in the profile of Southern New Hampshire University, when fully operational the distributed model is no longer a small college. It has moved away from the small college scale and educational mission and becomes an educational institution focused on customer service, market demand, educational integrity, and scale.

While the distributed university has multiple sites and delivers degrees in a variety of formats—from fully in-person to fully online—it is one institution. It centralizes services such as institutional and instructional technology, enrollment management, and financial aid. The centralization and integration of these services are designed to allow the campus to pursue new or growing markets at multiple locations without duplicating infrastructure.

Inherent Strengths of the Distributed University Model

The distributed university model is the most removed from the traditional model, and it is still the least utilized—although more institutions are embracing parts of this approach, few are able to adopt all aspects of the distributed model. The attraction of the distributed model is apparent: It is dynamic and market driven. The model is designed to be flexible and respond to current and emerging market trends. It utilizes technology in a way that lowers the cost of educational delivery. This combination of building enrollment and lowering the cost of delivery significantly aids financial stability.

Campuses in this model can be quite nimble, which can often help an institution be an early adopter in new program areas and in new regions. Since the infrastructure of market analysis and technology is already in place, the distributed model positions institutions for further expansion into new degree and certificate programs, with a reasonable likelihood of success. Their strong focus on customer service and responsiveness initially provides a student recruitment advantage, and can also secure early adopter status in high-demand markets.

The distributed university serves a significant and important educational mission. It provides access to higher education for many students who might not otherwise have the means or the opportunity to pursue college. Through its responsiveness to business and community needs, the distributed university can help ensure a return on investment for those same students.

Inherent Challenges of the Distributed University Model

The challenges of the distributed university model are significant. At inception, this approach requires heavy investment in marketing and sophisticated market analysis. For any campus, new programs do not automatically lead to greater enrollment; institutions using the distributed university model are fully dependent on new ventures paying dividends in enrollment and net revenue, and their market assessment must have a high degree of accuracy.

The distributed university model also requires significant infrastructure capacity, both in technology and in support systems. If a campus does not already have a robust technology system or has not already built the human and physical infrastructure to provide distance, online, and hybrid programs, this is a very significant and time-consuming investment.

These two requirements for success—sophisticated market analytics and well-developed and purpose-built infrastructure—can be a major barrier to entry for institutions seeking to move into the distributed university model. And once institutions have moved into the space successfully, they face a new challenge. While this model can help an institution become an early adopter of a new program or delivery model, if it is successful at tapping new markets its success can entice other, larger entities—particularly educational technology enterprises—to enter the market and pose direct competition.

For campuses that are evolving from a more traditional approach, the distributed university model represents a dramatic change in focus and purpose. For existing institutions that are place-based and have a long history of classroom teaching and face-to-face education, it is hard to overstate the dramatic shift in culture, educational systems, faculty and staff roles, and institutional purpose that this model demands.

And finally, this model runs counter to the traditional strengths of small colleges and universities. It challenges the assumption that small colleges are the setting for highly personalized learning in a residential campus community. In the process, this approach may challenge the identity of the institution itself.

A Contemporary Example of the Distributed University Model

The most visible, and arguably the most successful, current example of the distributed model is Southern New Hampshire University (SNHU). Unlike most independent colleges and universities, SNHU did not begin in the traditional model as a liberal arts college, although it was quite small for decades after it was established in the 1930s. It is the dramatic change in its direction, rapid growth, and the visibility of its work that make it a useful profile to consider in the context of small college transformation. Since the work of SNHU has been well documented elsewhere, this profile will consider the ways in which small independent colleges can learn from SNHU's evolution and the ways in which SNHU will likely remain unique.

SNHU is located in Manchester, New Hampshire. It began as a small independent school of accounting and secretarial science. The campus evolved in myriad ways through the middle of the last century, including acquiring programs from nearby campuses and expanding and changing its physical location. Never a particularly wealthy institution, by the early 2000s the university was struggling with enrollment and viability. It initially shored up its financial profile by building a strong online and continuing education portfolio. Initially, that online effort subsidized the core campus in essential ways. Ultimately, the online and hybrid programs grew so substantially that they outstripped the core campus and came to define the institution; however, the online function did not overwhelm the main campus. Instead, the online and on-campus programs each evolved, becoming more responsive and more dedicated to serving students in new ways. The success and visibility of SNHU's extended programs created benefits for the entire institution, and the main campus now has just over 3,000 students.

In total, today SNHU has over 93,000 undergraduate and graduate students. In addition to the main campus in Manchester, SNHU has 3 regional centers in New England (SNHU, n.d.c). The university offers more than 250 programs through a mixture of online, on-site, and hybrid options, with credentials ranging from certificates through the doctoral degree. Through College for America, SNHU provides low-cost degree programs designed for working adults using a competency-based approach and a flexible academic calendar (SNHU, n.d.a).

The story of SNHU is compelling. It illustrates the importance of focused and visionary leadership and the value of being an early adopter. The profile of SNHU also shows the degree of comprehensive change that would be necessary for most small independent colleges and universities to move into the distributed model.

PROFILE OF A DISTRIBUTED MODEL INSTITUTION: SOUTHERN NEW HAMPSHIRE UNIVERSITY

Field research and draft compilation of this campus profile conducted by Oscar R. Miranda Tapia while an EdM student at the Harvard Graduate School of Education

Brief History and Overview

As an institution that was once a small private college, SNHU does not have a typical history; although it was certainly quite small in its earlier iteration, its program offerings and founding are idiosyncratic. Founded by accountant Harry Alfred Benjamin "H.A.B." Shapiro in 1932, SNHU began as New Hampshire Accounting and Secretarial School, serving 42 students in bookkeeping, accounting, and secretarial courses (SNHU, n.d.b). Located in Manchester, New Hampshire, the program attracted traditional and non traditional students because it offered flexible enrollment and class time options like day and night classes. Moreover, the school's faculty also had workplace experience, a rarity among higher education faculty at the time. Beginning in 1941, as World War II swelled the ranks of military personnel at nearby Manchester Air Base, the school transitioned to educating active-duty military personnel in clerical skills during the day while they continued their duties at the base by night. The college would later open its doors to disabled veterans and, by the 1960s, the school offered 8-week courses across New England and Puerto Rico for military personnel. During this time, the school earned accreditation and was renamed New Hampshire College, offering associate and bachelor's degrees.

In the 1980s and 1990s, enrollment and course offerings expanded. As the American higher education landscape changed and workforce demands increased, the college was an early adopter of distance education and began offering its first online classes in 1995. Successful online courses led to more online offerings and, by the year 2000, the college's distance education program was recognized by the New England Association of Schools and Colleges as "cutting-edge." Enrollment grew rapidly to 8,000 students, largely because of the online programs. The college also began providing a 3-year bachelor's degree program that aimed to reduce costs for students and the college and was centered around competencies rather than courses. In 2001, the college was renamed SNHU.

SNHU's mission is to "transform the lives of learners" (SNHU, n.d.c). With just over 3,000 residential students and over 90,000 online students, SNHU is 1 of the fastest growing universities in the United States. According to President Paul LeBlanc, growth continues to be the priority for the institution, and SNHU plans to nearly triple the university's enrollment over the next 5 years. Currently, SNHU offers over 200 programs ranging from certificates to doctoral degrees in business, education, liberal arts, and STEM, among others.

SNHU and the Distributed University Model

Under the distributed University model, colleges and universities often create enrollment growth by developing branches beyond their home residential campus. Operating outside the traditional residential campus model, institutions may also use online education to provide high-demand programs that are driven by emerging markets. As higher education experiences major shifts in student demographics, college affordability, and expectations of college education, SNHU has responded not only by being market driven but also by developing a reach in both online education and branch campuses that positions it for nimbleness; it recognizes it will need to continue to adopt new programs that reach additional markets.

Three Market-Driven Initiatives

SNHU's online model is a prime example of an effort to reach a new market. Offering over 200 career-focused online degree programs, SNHU's online programs focus on educating working adults at a time when it is estimated that, by the year 2025, about 70% of new jobs will require a postsecondary degree. Since this program's inception, the university continues to innovate to add enrollment and reach. It has done so by adopting or expanding the following 3 initiatives over the last 10 years.

College for America

Launched in 2013, College for America (CfA) provides online competency and project-based degree programs for working adults who need higher education to advance in their careers. Established to meet labor market needs, CfA partners with over 120 employers nationwide across many industries including healthcare, business, government, retail, technology, and telecommunications. Tuition prices start at $5,000 a year with additional reimbursement discounts available through employers. Students may also qualify for federal financial aid to cover educational costs.

CfA begins with students choosing from an assortment of projects that require them to complete 1 to 8 workplace competencies aligned with the Lumina Foundation's Degree Qualifications Profile. Students need a total of 120 competencies to earn an associate degree, while a bachelor's degree requires 240 competencies. CfA programs are accessible 24/7, require no classes, and every student is assigned an adviser to support completion of the degree program. This flexibility makes the CfA program particularly appealing to working adults.

Degree in Three Program

Another initiative developed at SNHU in response to the market is the Degree in Three program. Degree in Three allows students to graduate with a Bachelor of Science degree in business in just 3 years, or 6 semesters (SNHU, n.d.d). The program is designed to help students save time and gain valuable skills; students spend 75% of their educational experience in the classroom and the last 25% in experiential learning practices outside the classroom. These out-of-class experiences may take the form of internships, seminars, team-based semester-long projects, and research, among other experiences, and the program is designed to make students more employable in a changing job market. Since its inception in 2011, student interest has been high, and the program has seen more than 50% yearly growth. Since the program can be completed in 3 years, students can save a quarter of the cost when compared to traditional 4-year undergraduate degrees.

SNHU's Advantage Program

The last innovative program the university offers is SNHU's Advantage program. Housed on a SNHU campus in Salem, New Hampshire, the Advantage program charges a flat rate of $10,000 per year as students seek an associate degree (SNHU, n.d.e). This is a marked reduction in cost from SNHU's main residential campus. Classes are taught by main campus professors and are only offered between 8:00 a.m. and 12:30 p.m., allowing students to still work full time. An incentive for program enrollment is that, after successful completion, students are automatically admitted to SNHU's on-campus undergraduate degree programs.

Process Toward Change

For over a decade, SNHU's strategy has yielded dramatic enrollment growth, achieved by providing convenient, affordable, and career-focused programs primarily for nontraditional students. In order to do so, SNHU has looked at models outside traditional higher education. The university evaluated external data from 2003 that predicted the demographic shifts in the traditional student population, including a major downturn in high school graduates, particularly in the Northeast. In response, SNHU turned its attention away from the traditional student market and instead focused on the 38 million working Americans with some college credit; no degree; and, quite often, student loans. By examining data from analytic software companies like Burning Glass Technologies and looking at broad-based job trends in conjunction with nuanced workforce needs, SNHU has expanded programming into high-demand fields. Organizations like the Institute for the Future in Palo Alto, California, and the Center for Creative Leadership in Greensboro, North Carolina, have aided SNHU when thinking about the next set of programs, courses, and delivery methods.

As SNHU continues to look beyond traditional higher education models, it has experienced a number of changes regarding curriculum revision and shared governance. One significant change was its pioneering effort to create direct assessment competency-based programs. This was the first client program of its kind, untethered to the traditional credit hour. For the Degree in Three program specifically, SNHU needed to find overlaps within the curriculum to achieve maximum efficiency.

These changes also brought about shifts in the governance structure. Within the university environment of shared governance, modifying the curriculum would prove challenging unless SNHU negotiated with traditional faculty members. SNHU wanted to experiment with many new things and to have a rapid response rate as new initiatives showed promise or failed to achieve their goals. In order to do so, the university created both a new governance structure and a physical separation for its online operations, giving them their own infrastructure, administrative systems, and governance process. In return, the leadership promised that if the online programs were successful, some of the additional revenue would help subsidize the main residential campus. Establishing these new efforts as revenue drivers outside of the usual systems created an opportunity for experimentation and relatively rapid development. It also involved considerable risk. Ultimately, the revenues from these market-driven initiatives have successfully supported the entire SNHU infrastructure, including the residential campus. According to campus leadership, getting some space from the usual shared governance model has been key to the success of the market-driven initiatives.

Timeline and Outcomes

Exploring and shifting to nontraditional higher education models has taken years at SNHU. It has required extensive research to ensure new methodologies would prove successful even though the campus was early to online education. Unlike most independent colleges of modest size, SNHU was unusually well positioned for responding to the 2008 recession, although the institution was not necessarily aware of it. The recession forced the university to spend $2 million from its reserves to expand marketing outside its region. This effort was so successful that SNHU approached the board the following year to ask for an additional $4 million that later resulted in an $11 million surplus. SNHU began its journey when there was a window of opportunity for online education, and competition in the online space for nonprofits was not as strong. SNHU took advantage of its unusual history and early adopter status and has maintained that position by ongoing growth.

When assessing the quality of its education, SNHU looks at several measures of success, including the more traditional forms such as graduate rates and persistence rates. But because of its unusual business model, SNHU uses unconventional measures as well. Most notable is the Net Promoter Score, a tool more commonly used to measure the customer experience in for-profit businesses. This tool allows SNHU to evaluate student satisfaction and loyalty to the university beyond traditional academic measures. The last measure of success is postgraduation employment rate, which is at 96%.

Conclusion

Over the last several years, SNHU has been consistently recognized as one of the most innovative schools in the nation. Its culture of extending beyond traditional higher education norms has been the result of an unusual history, strategic positioning, and aggressive commitment to change. President LeBlanc credits the institution's culture as one of the most important attributes. It is reinforced by its mission to transform the lives of learners. SNHU employees understand this, and when culture is cultivated in sync with vision, "it is incredibly powerful" (P. Le Blanc, personal interview, November 12, 2018).

Figure 8.1 Southern New Hampshire University at a glance.

Endowment	SNHU does not have an endowment
Student-to-Faculty Ratio	Overall, including online: 28:1 Traditional main campus: 14:1
Enrollment	93,000+
Four-Year Graduation Rate	49%
Six-Year Graduation Rate	56%
Key Elements of the Curriculum	Over 200 degree programs, offering programs on campus in Manchester, New Hampshire; online; or through competency-based degree program, CfA Curriculum includes prior learning assessment, project-based learning, and transfer support

Note: U.S. Department of Education (2017d) SNHU (n.d.c).

9

CHOOSING A PATH

As we have seen, the challenges facing small independent colleges and universities are significant. For most of these institutions, the question is not whether to adapt, but how to adapt. The taxonomy of approaches outlined in the preceding chapters provide a framework for understanding some of the options.

In the midst of responding to the shifts in the larger environment, campuses may be undertaking fundamental institutional changes that drive them, consciously or not, toward a different model. The taxonomy is a tool to help the leaders of colleges and universities make strategic decisions; to evaluate where their campus currently aligns; and to decide whether the path to institutional health and vitality can be found by remaining within that framework, or whether it is more strategic, and ultimately more sustainable, to move to a new model (Figure 9.1).

The five institutional models are not rigid. Many campuses may employ elements of several of the models but are predominantly in one model. For example, Dominican and Agnes Scott are in the distinctive program model, but in addition both campuses have added targeted new academic programs that diversify their offerings. Chapman is in the expansion model but retains a solid liberal arts core.

A Continuum of Change

In chapter 3 I suggested that the models can be placed within a continuum, from traditional to distributed. It is worth revisiting that framework in assessing what is involved in choosing a model.

In a broad sense, choosing a model requires a decision about the nature of change, and the impact of that change on the mission and culture of the campus. Institutions may choose to stay the course, which simply means

Figure 9.1 Continuum of change.

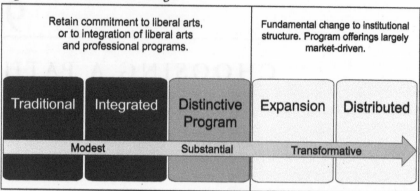

Note: Original graphic by Mary B. Marcy © 2019

making needed adaptations within their existing model. This is the path chosen by most of the campuses profiled in the traditional model and the integrated model: Colgate, Whitman, and California Lutheran. Staying the course does not mean the campus avoids change or adaptation; indeed, it is clear from the ambitious work these institutions have undertaken that significant change is underway and entirely possible while staying within the existing model. For example, Cal Lutheran became an HSI while staying within the integrated model. Whitman and Colgate both remain firmly within the traditional model while adding support for more defined career paths and developing programs to meet the needs of a more diverse student population. Such adaptions are designed to meet the needs of a changing student body and to respond to shifting expectations for higher education.

Campuses may also choose to move to a new model but retain fidelity to their mission and existing strengths. This is the path taken by Trinity, Dominican, Furman, and Agnes Scott. Their changes have been substantial and comprehensive but are still aligned with the campus's history, mission, and culture. In Trinity's case, the campus continued its mission of access to quality education for women. Dominican capitalized on its historic strength in community engagement and mentoring. Agnes Scott built part of the SUMMIT program around its excellence in international experiences. Furman derived the Furman Advantage from a long tradition of employing engaged learning practices. Each built on existing institutional strengths, while adopting a new model to respond to changing demographics and financial realities.

After evaluating the campus and the external environment, some institutions will elect to change their model and alter their mission in order to secure institutional sustainability. Such fundamental change means that the campus, at its core, has altered its approach to education in order to become more competitive or more viable. Such fundamental change is far reaching and comprehensive, shifting the entire focus of the institution; the campus will reach different students, through new programs, using a variety of educational delivery options, across multiple campus locations. This is the approach taken to some degree by Utica and Chapman, and more comprehensively by SNHU.

The Essential Questions

There are several essential questions that can help guide an institutional decision about which approach to adopt. Some of these questions are relevant for any strategic planning, while others are informed by the unusually challenging circumstances facing independent colleges and universities today. All involve honest institutional self-appraisal, clear data analysis, and a willingness to face the growing headwinds directly and strategically.

The Question of Mission

The first essential question is mission. What is our mission, are we currently enacting it, and how would a new approach affect the mission? More than a rhetorical question or one that is simply answered by a long-existing (but perhaps rarely referenced) mission statement, this is a question about the core values and culture of the institution. Who are the students and, given changing demographics, who are they likely to be? What are the enduring strengths of the campus? Do those strengths have relevance in the current higher education climate? It is essential to ask these questions, because, as we have seen, the path to sustainability may—or may not—embrace the traditional historic mission of the campus.

Similarly, it is important to be honest about the current mission when asking this question. I have noted earlier in this work that most small colleges and universities began as residential liberal arts institutions in the traditional model, but many are no longer in that space. But while program offerings may have evolved, the mission, at least as it is described, may have altered little. Many small campuses are liberal arts institutions in rhetoric only—their core offerings may not be enacting a commitment to liberal education or the primacy of liberal arts disciplines. Others have remained fiercely committed to liberal arts education in both word and action. Many small colleges also began with religious teaching at the heart of their mission. Whether and how this religious commitment remains is important to understand as the campus envisions its future. Still other institutions are committed to the education of a particular set of students, such as women's colleges and historically Black colleges and universities, and envisioning the future must include a discussion of that core mission.

Fidelity to mission will not, by itself, sustain a campus. The issue is whether—and if so, how—the campus can retain its mission while responding to the challenges of changing demographics, market forces, and fiscal realities. Choosing a path forward should include clarity about the ways in which the mission is currently being embraced (or not) and an equally honest evaluation of how the next stage of institutional evolution is likely to affect that mission. Both Colgate and Whitman found ways to respond to changing students and expectations while remaining true to their mission and liberal arts identity.

Some of the paths outlined here, such as the traditional model, the integrated model, and the distinctive program model, lend themselves to maintaining the historic mission of most small colleges and universities. Successful implementation involves adaptation and change but most likely will not alter the core mission of the campus. Others, such as the expansion model or the distributed university model, may call for enough changes to the institution's educational approach that it may affect aspects of the existing mission as well. This shift in mission could be the result, for example, of a discontinuation of most core liberal arts programs; involve a change from serving traditional college-age students to nontraditional students; or entail moving from a largely residential campus to a commuter, multicampus, or online institution.

The Question of the Challenge to Be Addressed

A second essential question concerns the reasons for choosing a particular model. What challenge or issue is the campus seeking to address with a new approach? There is no shortage of issues facing small colleges and universities. And, as we saw in earlier chapters, there are inherent strengths and inherent challenges in each model in the taxonomy. If the campus has great strength in the traditional liberal arts but has student recruitment challenges, it may consider moving to the integrated model in order to diversify its offerings. This is the approach taken by Trinity. A campus may adopt the distinctive program model to strengthen student recruitment and retention and enhance quality; this is the strategy embraced by Furman, Dominican, and Agnes Scott. If a campus has strong existing online programs or has a particular viable niche in its region, it may choose the expansion model, as Chapman and Utica have done.

In addressing challenges, if possible, the campus should also retain or build on institutional strengths. Over time and through ongoing faculty development and programmatic investment, most campuses develop a strong reputation in particular programs, or through distinctive pedagogical approaches. Small institutions, even those that consider themselves comprehensive universities, rarely have the breadth to offer a complete range of academic programs from the liberal arts to the preprofessional through the professional; inevitably some programs are more robust, and some programs typically found at larger institutions are quite modest or do not exist at all.

Identifying the issues to be addressed should not only inform the model to be adopted but also outline how success will be measured. Such measures might include increased enrollment, greater selectivity, improvement in retention and persistence to graduation, increased net tuition revenue, greater student postgraduation success, or institutional visibility. These measures not only provide a useful incentive for change but also offer a road map for the long-term health of the institution.

Because it often takes a number of years to successfully implement essential change, having markers of progress can provide energy for further change or serve as a useful point of reflection and correction if new initiatives do not yield the anticipated results. For example, as Dominican began implementing the Dominican Experience—but several years before it was fully established—graduation rates began to improve, initially modestly, and later dramatically. This substantial improvement was a useful proof of concept, reinforced the emerging institutional direction, and offered some ballast to the budget as the next set of changes toward the distinctive program model were implemented.

The Question of Students

A third major question for institutions to consider in choosing a model is the nature of its students. Specifically, the campus should ask who its students are and who they are likely to be given changing demographics. The first three models in this taxonomy—traditional, integrated, and distinctive program—are focused primarily, though not exclusively, on traditional-age college students. The last two models—expansion and distributed—tend to have a larger proportion of adult students, graduate students, part-time students, and returning degree seekers. The age and experiences of students should inform pedagogy, support systems, educational delivery systems, infrastructure, and the academic calendar.

Beyond the age of the students, campuses must consider the diversity of the current and emerging student body. Demographic trends clearly show that the number of traditional-age students is declining, particularly in some parts of the country. Further, traditional-age students are becoming increasingly diverse in race, ethnicity, and socioeconomic background. A growing percentage are the first in their family to attend college. If the goal of the campus is to continue to serve traditional-age students, then the path forward must embrace systems and practices that are likely to attract such students and are proven to help ensure their success. This reality informed Utica's decision to implement a tuition reset and informed Cal Lutheran's decision to become an HSI.

Knowing who their students are, and who their students are likely to be, is crucial to understanding the ways in which campuses can adapt. The landscape can vary considerably from one region of the country to another and from one institution to another. Most small colleges and universities have historically drawn students primarily from their region, with perhaps some extension beyond that area for specific high-profile programs. This regional perspective can help inform decisions about the most viable path forward. For example, as the number of high school graduates declines in many areas of the country, campuses may want to focus more on degree completion for adult students; however, this competitive market generally requires a change in the academic calendar and a robust technological infrastructure—adult students are often employed full time even as they pursue higher education, and they value the flexibility of online and hybrid programs. Identifying this as a priority market likely involves moving to the expansion or distributed model. Certainly SNHU provides a robust illustration of an institution that has reimagined itself to effectively serve more working adults.

Conversely, campuses where traditional-age students are more likely to be identified as first-generation or underrepresented students may be drawn to the integrated model, offering a broader array of programs tied more directly to the workplace. Or they may adopt the distinctive program model, with its commitment to high-impact educational practices and mentoring.

The Question of Resources

Of course, many small colleges and universities are already in difficult financial positions. That reality makes it essential to address the question of resources when determining a path forward. All the models are designed to support institutional viability, either by increasing the number of students, positioning the campus for greater selectivity, or diversifying program offerings. Identifying what investment is within the campus's capacity, and what model is most likely to lead to long-term sustainability, is crucial to success.

There are two types of investment to consider when evaluating the models. One is the investment of focused time. To be successful in developing an approach that will lead to improved quality and sustainability, the campus must commit its time and energy to defining and building the initiative. Just as it takes time to craft a comprehensive strategic plan, consciously adopting a model that will be successful involves ongoing, focused work over several years. Many of these approaches, for example, the distinctive program model, will require curriculum change. Other approaches, especially those focused on reaching a different student demographic, will require changes in support systems and structures. Certainly there can be markers of progress in the midst of the change, but the campus should evaluate how long it believes comprehensive change will take. For example, Cal Lutheran took eight years to become an HSI, but the improvements in community engagement, enrollment growth, and student success were felt throughout the process. Similarly, the creation of the Dominican Experience was a multiyear process, but early success in improving student persistence to graduation provided reinforcement for the approach, and support from key major donors fueled its ongoing development.

The second major investment to consider is the upfront investment of resources. The attraction of new programs or new models is real, but that attraction should not blind a campus to the equally real investment necessary to create and implement them with quality. This investment is often financial, whether building new buildings, adding faculty to create a new program, providing infrastructure support for new models of student advising and success, or investing in technology and faculty development to create more on line programs.

If a campus does decide to build new high-demand programs, then an analysis of the necessary investment, and expectations for the return on that investment, can guide the process. This analysis is essential when creating new programs that are not within existing strengths or are not easily supported by existing infrastructure. Building any new program with quality nearly always requires several years of lead time as the campus recruits new faculty and program leadership and develops the necessary infrastructure. In addition, many high-demand programs, such as those in the health sciences, require extensive specialized equipment and facilities. This means there is a significant commitment of money and time before the new program ever enrolls a student.

Chapman provides a good illustration of how a sophisticated analysis of market, campus capacity, and regional appetite for higher education can guide decisions about new programs and initiatives. Its strategic plan includes a detailed analysis of expected costs to begin programs, as well as the expected length of time for those programs to move to sustainability.

Because of the time and startup costs needed, the campus may also decide not to add new programs or may explore consortia and partnerships as ways to provide some offerings without such a significant initial financial investment. These ventures can also be complex and time consuming but are frequently less financially intensive. Some examples of this approach are illustrated in chapter 10.

The work of the development office should focus on these priorities, whether it is through a comprehensive campaign or in targeted fundraising. And the campus budget management needs to align with the long-term vision for the institution, not simply the usual year-over-year budget process. Understanding the campus's ability to raise money and shifting the institution's budget process to align with the long-term vision are essential processes that demand consistent implementation.

The Question of Leadership

The biggest challenge to realizing the promise of any of these models is the question of leadership. Because of the fierce and persistent headwinds facing small colleges and universities, there is a growing clamor for immediate answers, simple solutions, and heroic leadership. And indeed, some small colleges and universities do not believe they have the luxury of time to evaluate options. The process of adopting a model and realizing at least some progress does not have to take years. But lasting and sustainable change does take time, ongoing communication, consistent energy, and persistent and focused leadership.

Fundamentally changing the long-term prospectus for a campus and creating a hopeful and sustainable future is a comprehensive process, one that requires sustained leadership from the board, the president, and ultimately the campus. Changing curriculum, adapting systems to different students, or reaching a new market is challenging work at any time. To be implemented effectively, most of these models require the entire campus to grapple with issues of essential academic offerings, fiscal sustainability, staff and institutional capacity, changing student demographics, and student success. This means having regular conversations in large and small groups, engaging in ongoing research, and sharing data and information that are relevant to the future of the institution. All these processes require time and intellectual capital, but if done well, they are the keys to successful change.

What the successful institutions profiled in this book have in common is leadership that has been unwavering in its commitment to successfully implementing the approach that the campus has identified. A review of the transformation at SNHU is incomplete without recognizing the strong and unwavering leadership of a president and board who were clear about the need to become an online, customer-oriented institution. Similarly, Trinity survived because of a relentless commitment to serving the region; this commitment meant changing the programs and systems of the campus to embrace, rather than deny or avoid, the diverse community in which it is located.

In each case, strategic investments, presidential and board leadership, or philanthropic support were leveraged to bring about longer term change and advance the larger vision. Such focus requires that campuses not try everything at once but instead recognize the importance and primacy of the central vision. Effective leadership also brings the campus community together, beyond the day-to-day work, to make consistent progress on a larger goal.

The ability to maintain fidelity to a long-term vision while navigating the challenges of ongoing campus work is fundamental to success in adopting a new model. Embracing and celebrating short-term progress on the way to the larger vision can provide reinforcement and energy for the long-term path to quality and sustainability.

Using Essential Questions to Guide Decision-Making and Lead Change

If fundamental change is necessary, the campus should consider how to engage key shared governance constituencies throughout the process. In the institutions profiled earlier in this book, it is notable that some fully embraced shared governance, while others worked outside of the conventional governance processes to generate new revenue and bring about change. In all cases, internal and external stakeholders were constantly engaged, while campus leadership provided data, analysis, and information to inform decision-making.

The questions outlined in this chapter should not be conducted only by the leadership team or by one constituent group but developed through broader conversations. Such a process provides crucial information about the time, resources, and energy required to undertake fundamental change and do so with quality and in a sustainable manner. This process involves ongoing engagement of internal and external stakeholders and candid information sharing—information about the institution's current status and about the headwinds of demography, expectations, and fiscal sustainability outlined earlier. It should also include current research that focuses on student learning and student success and a realistic appraisal of the campus's current and prospective student population.

By sharing common data, research, and information, each constituency can then provide necessary insight for adopting a path forward. Faculty, of course, should evaluate new programs and institutional change processes with an eye toward academic integrity, pedagogical approaches, and faculty development. Staff will have the background to evaluate, for example, whether the campus's technology infrastructure can support off-campus programs or whether existing personnel can offer appropriate support to a new constituency, such as adult students. Students can provide insight about their current experiences and reactions to the vision for the future. The board should assess for long-term viability, mission, and institutional positioning and ultimately provide financial support to help the vision become reality. Fundamental change, such as developing a distinctive program, requires ongoing campus discussion over multiple semesters as programs, student needs, and external appetite are evaluated and integrated. Institutional transformation, such as that usually necessary to adopt the distributed model, requires a clear discussion of the institution's current path and the potential benefits of undertaking holistic transformation of the institution.

This summary of the essential questions can help frame campus discussion, invites the participation of all constituencies in shared governance, and requires both data and institutional memory to determine the path ahead.

IO

GOING IT ALONE? THE EVOLVING ROLE OF CONSORTIA AND PARTNERSHIPS

The models for sustainability and innovation presented in this book frame options for independent colleges and universities as freestanding institutions. They can also effectively position an institution for exploring consortial arrangements and new types of partnerships. And partnerships and consortia can, in turn, provide additional innovative ways to manage cost and develop new opportunities and programs.

Refining an institution's strategy through commitment to a particular model and strategic plan creates a clear focus. This institutional focus provides a means to evaluate potential partnerships based on their alignment with the long-term vision for the campus. The models outlined in this book enhance a campus's ability to strategically explore consortia and partnerships to create new programs, enhance student opportunity, and secure financial and programmatic efficiencies.

In recent years, significant changes to the usual consortial arrangements we have long associated with small colleges have emerged. New types of partnerships are also in development. Both are changing in ways that reward the clarity of vision and innovation represented by these models.

There are two broad ways in which campuses are increasing the breadth and depth of options for students while maintaining fidelity to their mission and strategic vision: through an evolving notion of consortia and through an increasingly sophisticated exploration of institutional partnerships.

The Evolving Uses of Consortia

Consortial arrangements have been established among independent colleges and universities for a number of years. Historically, the most robust consortia have been among institutions in close geographic proximity. They may cross-register courses, share cocurricular programming, collaborate on academic services such as library and learning management systems, and share security and transportation services. The Claremont Colleges in California and the Five Colleges in Massachusetts are good examples of this approach. The collaboration feeds cross-institutional development and allows the campuses to realize considerable economies of scale for many basic services and programs. For example, another consortium, Colleges of the Fenway, includes five institutions that are all located within one square mile in the city of Boston. By sharing contracts, services, and intramural activities, these colleges realize an annual savings, collectively, of approximately $2.5 million per year (C. Ramsbottom, personal interview, September 17, 2018).

Less extensive consortia have also developed through an alignment of educational interests and values. Some, such as the New American Colleges and Universities group cited earlier in this book, align based on a particular educational approach. Their research and meetings focus on professional development and shared educational programs or aspirations. Such consortia are less concerned with back office functions and economies of scale. Instead, they provide access to research and information that are particularly useful for their type of institution. They may also share best practices and provide focused professional development.

Still other groups are perhaps too loosely configured to formally be considered consortia but are organized enough to provide some economic and political leverage for small colleges, allowing a group of institutions to bid on contracts, share services, or realize back office efficiencies. Such consortia may also represent the common interests of independent colleges to state and federal governments. Consortia that share contract bidding and some services are found across the nation. The work is often coordinated through a statewide office that provides some economies of scale for independent colleges that are too small to secure similar negotiating leverage on their own.

While these consortial arrangements have been in existence for some time, a different set of consortia is just beginning to emerge; only recently have they begun to take new and more nimble forms. The new approaches are less constrained by physical proximity. Instead, they use educational technology and a shared purpose to support integrated approaches. They are usually aligned around an effort to provide an education that is more financially accessible for students and more fiscally sustainable for their campuses. Often, they are using the consortium to offer new, high-demand programs that would be practically or financially prohibitive to offer for a single campus.

A good example of such an emerging consortium is the Lower Cost Models for Independent Colleges Consortium (LCMC). Established in 2017, the group is still in its infancy but has already received support from the Davis Educational Fund and the Bill and Melinda Gates Foundation. It took three years to move from conception to launch, and initial foundation funding was essential to establishing the group (M. Alexander, personal interview, March 25, 2019). Together, these campuses pursue a shared mission: to improve instructional quality, and to make college more affordable at institutions with a large number of low-income students (Lasell University, 2017).

The 20 member institutions of the LCMC are geographically dispersed, from Massachusetts to California and many states in between; they all have a significant number of Pell-eligible students. Their work uses technology and shared expertise to add programs that—due to the cost and specialized expertise required—would be difficult to develop independently for any of the member institutions. The LCMC is focused on two objectives: to support one another by sharing information and overcoming impediments and to develop programs together that can be delivered from a centralized location, but are accessible to students throughout the consortium (M. Alexander, personal interview, March 25, 2019).

While all the LCMC consortial campuses have the liberal arts as an essential component of their own educational models, their initial academic collaboration is focused on courses in two academic programs well outside of the liberal arts mainstream: financial planning and computer science. The programs are delivered online, and students are supported by faculty at their home campus. These are program areas with high student demand, but they can be expensive to launch, time consuming to develop, and difficult to maintain for a single small campus. The cost to students is 30% to 50% lower for these shared courses than those delivered in the usual manner (M. Alexander, personal interview, March 25, 2019).

Another new consortial approach involves collaboration using a shared third-party content provider. This is the strategy used by a group of eight institutions who have developed new courses in partnership with Google. In this consortium, Google has created the curriculum, content, and materials for courses in computer science and data science. The eight participating small colleges provide campus-based support for students, including faculty leadership for projects. Like the LCMC, the campuses involved are scattered across the country (it is worth noting that some campuses participate in both consortia cited here). They have developed the program arrangement to provide additional high-demand courses for students in areas where they lack the infrastructure, faculty expertise, or both (J. Docking, personal interview, March 6, 2019).

On a larger scale, the Council of Independent Colleges has developed the CIC Online Course Sharing Consortium to serve essentially as a matchmaker, aligning supply and demand among its member institutions. The Online Course Sharing Consortium leverages existing online programs and provides more streamlined access to courses for students across campuses.

CIC's innovative approach uses technology to match student needs with institutional capacity. All member institutions of CIC, more than 700 in number, are eligible to enroll. The consortium serves as a broker of sorts, identifying excess capacity in online programs at member campuses and offering those spaces to students at other member campuses who need the course(s) for their degree requirements. Through the consortium, campuses can be either a home institution or a teaching institution. Home institutions use the consortium to provide courses that are necessary for their students to stay on track for a degree but may have low enrollment or are not offered every semester on their own campus. Meanwhile, teaching institutions have online capacity and offer available spaces to the home institutions. Course content and learning outcomes are shared in advance to ensure the seamless transfer of credits. The home institution receives regular tuition from the student and gives a portion of that tuition to the teaching institution.

The CIC Online Course Sharing Consortium addresses several significant issues: It reduces the number of low-enrollment courses on home campuses, fills vacant slots on teaching campuses, adds revenue to both home and teaching campuses, and keeps students on path to their degrees. By building the consortium from the existing membership of CIC, campuses can be assured that the educational philosophy of the institution that is delivering needed credits is largely in alignment with the home campus.

There are several characteristics of these emerging consortia that differentiate them from the older models. Most apparent is that they all use technology to link campuses in geographically disparate parts of the country. This approach allows for greater opportunities to develop consortia based on shared institutional needs and interests and avoids the direct competition often experienced by campuses in close geographic proximity. In addition, unlike more traditional consortia, they are not deeply entangled through back office services and instead have developed their consortia primarily around academic programs. They supplement existing offerings on campuses but do not challenge the independence of the institutions. These consortia are still in their infancy and at present provide collaboration on only a few courses. But they represent an intriguing new way to approach consortia, one enabled by, but not controlled by, technology.

Like earlier consortia, these approaches continue to leverage economies of scale but focus more on the academic core than on business services. They have found that, when seeking external support, either through foundations or through for-profit companies, both the profile of students and the number of students reached are important. For example, the LCMC describes their consortia as serving "more than 35,000 students," and the Google initiative was developed after outreach to the entire Council of Independent Colleges membership base (J. Docking, personal interview, March 6, 2019). Small campuses are finding that economies of scale are still important aspects of consortia. In an earlier era, they provided leverage through business office functions and physical proximity. Today, economies of scale are equally important in securing arrangements with major outside entities; some because of their commitment to expanding educational access, others because of their need for a supply of college graduates with particular skills.

The Changing Approach to Academic Partnerships

Another way in which small colleges are adapting is by broadening their approach to institutional partnerships. An expanded view of partnerships can provide new opportunities for strengthening the academic program and increasing fiscal sustainability, especially at smaller institutions that cannot provide a full range of programs and support on their own.

These partnerships are more creative and often more ambitious than the conventional list of internships and practicum. They are unusual because they challenge us to move beyond the old notion that we must operate independently—"each tub on its own bottom"—in order to retain fidelity to mission and quality. That is an outdated, narrow view of institutional identity and of academic integrity, one that can lead us to dismiss new opportunities of genuine significance.

In recent years, my own campus has undertaken several new partnerships while evaluating their alignment with mission and their potential for increasing student opportunity and fiscal sustainability. The most innovative new partnership Dominican has developed is our engagement with Make School, a technology academy. It represents a fundamentally different way for us to provide new curricular offerings and holds considerable promise for our students and faculty. It is also a significantly different approach to delivering parts of our curriculum and has involved tremendous ongoing effort and evaluation.

Prior to our partnership, Make School was a freestanding unaccredited campus in San Francisco focused on technology skills such as web design, coding, and app development. Dominican does not have a computer science program. Our faculty and students were hungry for the opportunity to develop skills in digital literacy and design, as well as coding capabilities.

The resulting partnership draws on the strengths and knowledge of each institution. Dominican's established faculty are providing general education courses to Make School students, and Make School's professionally skilled faculty are delivering computer science courses on the Dominican campus. Make School retains its identity, and its degree is accredited through an incubation relationship with Dominican; its enrolled students can earn a bachelor's of science degree in applied computer science. The result is a new bachelor's of science degree in applied computer science delivered on the Make School campus in San Francisco, and new computer science courses, up to a minor, delivered at Dominican's campus in Marin County. Dominican's native students can take courses across the curriculum in computer science and related areas (regardless of major), and faculty can augment their programs, courses, and expertise by partnering with Make School faculty.

The evaluation of this potential partnership involved in-depth discussion of alignment with our mission and our goals. Specifically, we knew that any potential partnership had to align with our distinctive program, the Dominican Experience. We also knew the pedagogical approach of faculty and commitment to student success needed to be compatible, even before we began discussions.

We were impressed with Make School's diversity of students and faculty engagement. Their approach to pedagogy, curriculum, and cocurriculum had surprising and reassuring parallels to our own. The quality of the program, dedication of the faculty, and diversity of the students convinced us that the partnership was worth pursuing. Our faculty, members of the senior leadership team, and members of our board of trustees met multiple times with our Make School counterparts. The faculty ultimately approved the program by an 85% margin; the board of trustees unanimously approved the partnership. This led to a successful accreditation process for the new program through our accrediting agency, the WASC Senior College and University Commission. Accreditation ensured our programs are aligned, have academic integrity and appropriate controls, and deliver the promised new opportunities for our students and faculty. In this case accreditation was a substantial aid to innovation.

This is a dramatically different venture that has challenged our creativity and inspired our sense of possibility. Dominican is long established, and Make School is just beyond its start-up phase. Dominican is nonprofit, with a conventional high-tuition, high-aid student funding model; Make School is for-profit, with an income share agreement. Dominican plans its curriculum, calendar, and requirements years in advance, and Make School has been adapting to the needs of a fast-changing market. Ultimately, what made the partnership a reality was the realization that we share a deep commitment to the goals and vision behind the Dominican Experience and to the external evaluation of our accreditor. While the structure of our programs was different, our missions and the students we were serving were not so far apart.

The Dominican–Make School partnership provides technology courses beyond our internal capacity, and in turn it highlights the deep need for a strong general education for students entering the technology professions. The arrangement also provides exposure to new networks and businesses for both campuses. Through the partnership, we have created a means of providing these opportunities without investing in a new (and likely siloed) academic discipline at Dominican and without investing in additional infrastructure and programs on-site at Make School. Each party will provide programs and support in the ways we do exceptionally well, fully in alignment with our missions.

Another new approach to partnerships is being developed at Lasell University in Newton, Massachusetts. Through the new initiative Lasell Works, students are experiencing more applied learning while lowering the cost of their education.

Through this initiative, new students at Lasell can choose to enroll in the campus's regular degree offerings or enroll in the Lasell Works program. Students in Lasell Works have a guided pathway through college, spending their second year off campus while enrolling in online courses. During this year, students maintain part-time employment. These job opportunities are the crux of their innovative partnership: The jobs are identified by the university, working with local businesses and nonprofits, to align student abilities and business needs.

While the students are working in their second year, they are also taking online classes at Lasell. Both the number of hours worked and the number of credits students can take during their employment are limited by the university to promote student success. Student employment is linked to a professional development seminar taught at the university, thus tying the external partnerships and student experience into their academic program.

While some aspects of Lasell Works recall earlier models of co-op experiences at institutions such as Antioch College or Northeastern University, Lasell is using partnerships and technology in intriguing new ways. And the program is explicitly designed to reduce the cost of college, a major concern for students and families. The goal is to leverage external partnerships and technology to lower the price for students, all while ensuring they have a fully integrated educational experience.

The cost of tuition actually goes down each year a student in Lasell Works is at the institution. This is accomplished by spreading the savings of the second year—the time when students are working and enrolled online—across the remaining two years of the program. The design was structured to further incentivize students to complete their degrees. The declining tuition rate for students entering the Lasell Works program in 2019 meant that they could expect to pay $39,000 in tuition their first year, $33,000 in their second year, $29,000 in their third year, and $27,000 in the fourth year. The university estimates a 4-year savings of $22,000 to $38,000 for a student pursuing a bachelor's degree (Lasell University, 2019; M. Alexander, personal interview, March 25, 2019).

Evaluating Consortia and Partnerships

There are five key questions that can aid in the evaluation of a potential consortium agreement or new partnership. The first, of course, is: why? Effective partnerships take time, focus, and often financial investment, so the anticipated value, and timeline for realizing that value is essential to determining whether to pursue an opportunity.

The second essential question: Does the potential partnership align with institutional mission and strategic direction—does it reinforce the model we want to adopt as a campus? If the answer is no, then the partnership is probably a distraction and not a fit for the institution. Ideally the partnership will leverage and support larger institutional change. Lasell Works is a good example of a partnership that was an ideal fit for the campus: President Michael Alexander had made college affordability a central goal of his leadership several years before the program was established.

The third essential question: What is the likely effect of a given partnership on student success and academic integrity? For example, when we began exploring Dominican's partnership with Make School, this question was at the heart of the discussion. A commitment to align with a for-profit technology school could only work if our commitment to student success and academic legitimacy were at the forefront of our negotiations.

The fourth question: What is the necessary level of investment in time, focus, staff and faculty commitment, and financial resources? Some partnerships and consortia, such as the CIC Online Course Sharing Consortium, may provide clear benefits for a limited investment. Others may take considerable time and resources over multiple years; in these cases, the alignment and potential benefits must be clear.

The final question: Is the level of risk involved in establishing the partnership fully understood? Risk in this sense is not only about the likelihood of success for the effort, but also reputational risk, as well as the cost of distraction and movement away from other core efforts.

There is no simple way to evaluate a potential partnership or consortial arrangement; they are complex arrangements and demand sophisticated thinking from key stakeholders across an institution. But such arrangements can be worth the effort. They offer intriguing new ways to address some of the core challenges of cost, market, and distinctiveness facing small colleges and universities. The examples presented here are an introduction to a growing set of innovations. As institutions continue to grapple with the headwinds they face, such arrangements are likely to proliferate.

I n the last few years unanticipated closures and revelations of severe financial difficulties have emanated from a number of small colleges and universities. These announcements have led to heightened media scrutiny and widespread anxiety in the sector. Unfortunately, the intensity of this anxiety has made it difficult to separate fact from hyperbole. While the most extreme cases that make headlines may not be fully representative, it is nonetheless apparent that the story of fiscal austerity is a reality at many, if not most, small colleges and universities. And the desire to find a path forward that is both financially sustainable and academically responsible is manifest. At a time of great anxiety and considerable ferment in small colleges and universities, it is reassuring to realize there are viable options for change, and many creative ways to adapt to the challenging environment. This book is an attempt to frame those options in a useful manner, to help these campuses respond with both information and creativity to the many demands they face.

Aside from the rare luxury of already holding significant institutional wealth, there is no simple solution or magic bullet to address the challenges of small colleges and universities. Change and innovation are needed to meet the concerns of the present, and to face the rising challenges of the future. It is encouraging to note that, more than is typically reported, change and innovation are indeed happening at many campuses. This book captures the nature of these innovations through the development of a broad taxonomy of strategic change at small colleges and universities. In the process, it provides an assessment of the application and effectiveness of a range of approaches in different institutional settings.

Because small colleges are undergoing substantial pressure and facing considerable challenges, the sector is also alive with ideas for new approaches and creative responses to the difficulties these campuses encounter. Along with the taxonomy of approaches to institutional focus that encompasses the bulk of this text, some of the more intriguing emergent ideas are outlined in the chapter on new types of partnerships and consortia. Because these ideas are still in development, it is difficult to predict which presage fundamentally new ways to organize and offer independent higher education, and which will prove to be less viable. The fact that a number of institutions are trying creative and different approaches to educational delivery, and that they are using technology to highlight, rather than replace, their highly personalized style of education, suggests that at least some of these efforts will become more mainstream.

Regardless of the approach adopted, these innovations take time to evaluate, to develop, and to implement. Small colleges do not have the luxury of adopting the Silicon Valley motto to "fail faster." It takes capital to fail faster, and—in the language of another current idiom—it takes time to pivot to new modes of teaching, learning, and delivering education. While there is considerable demand for dramatic and urgent change, comprehensive change on an institutional scale still needs to be considered, sustainable, and aligned with the capacity of the institution.

Thus, while there is no silver bullet, there are consistent themes across these campuses. Evaluation of these strategies shows recurrent patterns for successful adaptation. Institutions that successfully adapt to the rapidly shifting environment and implement fundamental change begin with a clear assessment of the campus's current position and a willingness to embrace a strategic path to the future. They maintain clarity about their goal and honesty within their own campus about what will be required to meet that goal. They demand steady leadership from the board, the president, and the senior team. They require a willingness to take strategic, but not foolhardy, risks. And they require resilience and a recognition that the great strength of most institutions is not nimbleness or entrepreneurship, but a commitment to education in its broadest sense—as a path to opportunity and a means of social and personal advancement. They also recognize that to secure this strength for the future requires significant adaptation, as the environment within which these campuses operate is undergoing dramatic change.

The challenges to the core business model for small colleges remain persistent, even as campuses employ the new approaches outlined in this book. Tuition resets, more strategic approaches to student recruitment, cost control, and maximizing nontuition revenue do not change the core model of high tuition coupled with high financial aid, they simply reposition within that model. A few new ideas, such as the income share agreement described in Dominican's partnership with Make School or the Lasell Works approach, are somewhat more disruptive to the standard business model, but they are far from being fully tested or easily adopted by multiple institutions. Perhaps these experiments will lead to fundamentally different strategies for financing small colleges and universities. But perhaps high tuition and high financial aid are—to paraphrase a thought about democracy attributed to Winston Churchill—the worst possible way to finance independent higher education, except for all the others.

The diversity of the United States' system of higher education has long been touted as one of our nation's greatest strengths, and the small college or university founded with a focus on the liberal arts is one of the distinctive American contributions to higher education. While the individual institutions are modest in size, there is more to recommend them than simply the oft-cited cry of Daniel Webster referring to Dartmouth that "it is a small college, but there are those who love it." There are over 700 independent colleges and universities in the United States. Many have been in existence for well over a century, with a long list of accomplished and successful alumni. They often serve as anchor institutions for their region, providing economic vitality and educational opportunity where there are few other means to access these resources. Most retain a commitment to a mission-focused education that reaches beyond workforce preparation to encompass the skills needed to craft a meaningful and ethical life. It is apparent that the mission of these institutions is important to continuing to provide student access and success in American higher education. That need will only grow as the student population continues to become more racially, ethnically, and socioeconomically diverse.

Indeed, as our nation becomes more diverse, the opportunities provided by small colleges and universities become more essential. These campuses, with their capacity to respond to individual student needs and their commitment to an enduring notion of learning that moves beyond simply the functional to critical thinking, are at the core of a more hopeful future for both individuals and our society. To provide that opportunity, they need to secure their own futures as well. This book is one attempt to help them do so.

REFERENCES

Agnes Scott College. (n.d.a). *Endowment*. Retrieved from https://www.agnesscott .edu/thegreatnessbeforeus/questions-answered/endowment.html

Agnes Scott College. (n.d.b). *Mission and values*. Retrieved from https://www .agnesscott.edu/about/mission-values/index.html

Agnes Scott College. (2018, September 20). *U.S. News ranks Agnes Scott College no. 1 most innovative school in the country*. Retrieved from https://www.agnesscott.edu/ news/archive/2018/09/usnewsandworld2018.html

Agnes Scott College. (2019). *SUMMIT: The Agnes Scott College experience*. Retrieved from https://www.agnesscott.edu/summithub/

Association of American Colleges & Universities. (2014). *Institute on high-impact practices and student success*. Retrieved from https://www.aacu.org/summerinstitutes/ hips/2014

Association of American Colleges & Universities. (2015, January 20). *Falling short? College learning and career success selected findings from online surveys of employers and college students*. Washington DC: AAC&U and Hart Research Associates. Retrieved from https://www.aacu.org/leap/public-opinion-research/2015-survey-results

Association of American Colleges and Universities. (2019). *Raising our voices: Reclaiming the narrative on the value of higher education—Annual meeting, 2019*. Retrieved from https://www.aacu.org/AM19

Astin, Alexander W. (1997). *What matters in college? Four critical years revisited*. San Francisco, CA: Jossey-Bass.

Bard College. (2019). *The Bard College language and thinking program*. Retrieved from http://languageandthinking.bard.edu/about/

Barr, Robert B., & Tagg, John. (1995). From teaching to learning—A new paradigm for undergraduate education. *Change: The Magazine of Higher Learning, 27*(6), 12–26.

Barry, Martin, and Barry, Justin. (1984). *A brief history of Dominican College of San Rafael*. Dominican University of California Library Archives.

California Lutheran University. (n.d.a). *About Cal Lutheran: Facts at a glance*. Retrieved from https://www.callutheran.edu/about/quick-facts.html

California Lutheran University. (n.d.b). *Info for Latinx STEM grads*. Retrieved from https://www.callutheran.edu/offices/institutional-research/

California Lutheran University. (2018). *Annual report, 2017–18*. Retrieved from https://www.callutheran.edu/president/annual-report/2017-2018/

Casey, Brian W. (2018). *Colgate University's third century: A vision statement*. Hamilton, NY: Colgate University.

Chapman University. (n.d.a). *Engineering the future: Strategic plan for Chapman University 2019–2023*. Orange, CA: Chapman University.

Chapman University. (n.d.b). *Our story*. Retrieved from https://www.chapman.edu/about/our-story/index.aspx

Chapman University. (n.d.c). *Previous 5-year strategic plans*. Retrieved from https://www.chapman.edu/about/our-family/leadership/strategic-plan/previous.aspx

Chapman University. (2016). *Chapman University factbook 2015–2016*. Retrieved from https://www.chapman.edu/campus-services/institutional-research/_files/FactBook-files/2015-COMPLETE.pdf

Chapman University. (2017). *Fostering a diverse and inclusive campus culture: Strategic plan for diversity and inclusion*. Orange, CA: Chapman University.

Chopp, Rebecca. (2013). Against the grain: Liberal arts in the 21st century. In Chopp, R. S., Frost, S., & Weiss, D. H. (Eds.), *Remaking college: Innovation and the liberal arts*. Baltimore, MD: Johns Hopkins University Press.

Colgate University. (n.d.a). *Academic majors and minors: Courses of study concentrations*. Retrieved from http://www.colgate.edu/academics/majors-and-minors

Colgate University. (n.d.b). *Brian W. Casey: The 17th president of Colgate University*. Retrieved from https://www.colgate.edu/about/people-of-colgate/president-brian-w-casey

Colgate University. (n.d.c). *Liberal arts core curriculum*. Retrieved from https://www.colgate.edu/academics/core-curriculum

Colgate University. (n.d.d). *Residential life at Colgate University*. Retrieved from https://www.colgate.edu/campus-life/residential-life

Colgate University (n.d.e). *What's in a name? Colgate's origins and evolution*. Retrieved from https://200.colgate.edu/looking-back/moments/whats-name-colgates-origins-and-evolution

Colgate University. (2018a). *Colgate at 200 years*. Retrieved from https://200.colgate.edu/looking-forward/vision/colgate-at-200-years

Colgate University. (2018b). *Common data set 2018–2019*. Retrieved from https://www.colgate.edu/sites/default/files/inline-files/CDS-18-19.pdf

Colgate University. (2014). *Strategic plan: Living the liberal arts in our third century*. Hamilton, NY: Colgate University.

Colgate University. (1993). *Colgate University mission statement*. Retrieved from https://www.colgate.edu/about/university-mission-statement

College Board, The. (n.d.). *Southern New Hampshire University profile*. Retrieved from https://bigfuture.collegeboard.org/college-university-search/southern-new-hampshire-university

College Board, The. (2018). *Trends in college pricing 2018: Average net price, private nonprofit four-year*. Retrieved from https://trends.collegeboard.org/college-pricing/figures-tables/average-net-price-over-time-full-time-students-private-nonprofit-four-year-institutions

Colorado College. (2019). *The block plan*. Retrieved from https://www.coloradocollege.edu/basics/blockplan/

Council of Independent Colleges, The. (2018). *Innovation and the Independent College*. Retrieved from https://www.cic.edu/r/r/innovations-report/Documents/CIC-Innovations-SecuringOurFuture.pdf

Council of Independent Colleges, The. (2019a). *Members of CIC*. Retrieved from https://www.cic.edu/about/members

Council of Independent Colleges, The. (2019b). *Leading strategic change: 2019 president's institute conference*. Retrieved from https://www.cic.edu/programs/2019-Presidents-Institute

Data USA. (2019). *Utica College profile*. Retrieved from https://datausa.io/profile/university/utica-college/

Dewey, J. (1933). *How we think: A restatement of the relation of reflective thinking to the educative process*. Boston, MA: D. C. Heath.

Dominican University of California. (2017). *Institutional report for reaffirmation submitted to the WASC Senior College and University Commission*. San Rafael, CA: Dominican University of California.

Dominican University of California. (2019). *The Dominican experience*. Retrieved from https://www.dominican.edu/about/the-dominican-experience

Earlham College. (2019). *Community with a difference: Principles and practices*. Retrieved from http://earlham.edu/student-life/#panel-50984

Evangelauf, Jean. (April 6, 1994). A new "Carnegie classification." *The Chronicle of Higher Education*. Retrieved from https://www.chronicle.com/article/A-New-Carnegie/91088

Furman University. (n.d.). *The Furman advantage: A four-year pathway*. Retrieved from: https://www.furman.edu/furman-advantage/

Gallup-Purdue. (2014). *Life in college matters for life after college: The 2014 Gallup-Purdue index report*. Washington DC: Gallup.

Guskin, Alan E., & Marcy, Mary B. (2003). Dealing with the future now: Principles for creating a vital campus in a climate of restricted resources. *Change: The Magazine of Higher Learning, 35*(4), 10–21.

Hannon, Kerry. (November 2, 2018). More colleges are playing the long game. *New York Times*. Retrieved from https://www.nytimes.com/2018/11/02/education/learning/colleges-universities-career-services.html

Hill, Catharine B., & Davidson Pisacreta, Elizabeth. (2019). *The economic benefits and costs of a liberal arts education*. New York, NY: Andrew W. Mellon Foundation and Ithaka S+R. Retrieved from https://mellon.org/media/filer_public/82/fa/82fac4d2-8e1c-4b7e-ba80-5efbd396c6c9/catharine_hill_on_economic_outcomes_1-9-2019.pdf

Horn, Michael B. (2019). *Choosing college: How to make better learning decisions throughout your life*. San Francisco, CA: Jossey-Bass.

Kalamazoo College. (2019). *The K plan*. Retrieved from https://www.kzoo.edu

Keller, George. (2004). *Transforming a college: The story of a little-known college's strategic climb to national distinction*. Baltimore, MD: Johns Hopkins University Press.

Kovacs, Kasia. (October 6, 2016). Real-world experience and the liberal arts. *Inside Higher Education*. Retrieved from https://www.insidehighered.com/news/2016/10/05/furman-u-guarantees-internships-research-opportunities-and-mentors-each-student

Kuh, G. D., O'Donnell, K., & Reed, S. D. (2013). *Ensuring quality and taking high-impact practices to scale*. Washington DC: Association of American Colleges & Universities.

Kuh, G. D., & Schneider, C. G. (2008). *High-impact educational practices: What they are, who has access to them, and why they matter*. Washington DC: Association of American Colleges & Universities.

Lapovsky, Lucie. (2019, April). *Do price resets work?* Retrieved from https://lapovsky.com/wp-content/uploads/2010/07/Do-Price-Resets-Work-.pdf

Lasell University. (2017, October 4). *Lower Cost Models for Independent Colleges Consortium (LCMC) receives Gates Foundation support*. Retrieved from https://www.Lasell.edu/discover-Lasell/news/lower-cost-models-for-independent-colleges-consortium-receives-gates-foundation-support.html

Linfield College. (2019). *Evenstad Center for Wine Education home page*. Retrieved from https://www.linfield.edu/wine.html

Marcy, Mary B. (2017a). Beyond mere survival: Transforming independent colleges and universities. *Change: The Magazine of Higher Learning, 49*(3), 36–44.

Marcy, Mary B. (2017b). *The small college imperative: From survival to transformation*. Washington DC: Association of Governing Boards of Universities and Colleges.

Mintz, Steven. (2014, April 2). Four emergent higher education models [blog post]. Retrieved from https://www.insidehighered.com/blogs/higher-edgamma/four-emergent-higher-education-models

Murray, Kathleen M. (2015). *Presidential installation address: The frontier of the liberal arts*. Walla Walla, WA: Whitman College. Retrieved from https://www.whitman.edu/installation/presidential-address

National Research Center for College & University Admissions, The. (2016). *Major group trend 2016-2022*. Data from WICHE and Encoura Data Lab by ACT.

New American Colleges and Universities, The. (n.d.). *Mission statement*. Retrieved from https://newamericancolleges.org/

Pascarella, E. T., & Blaich, C. (2013). Lessons from the Wabash study of liberal arts education. *Change: The Magazine of Higher Learning, 45*(2), 6–15.

Pascarella, E. T., & Terenzini, P. T. (1991). *How college affects students*. San Francisco, CA: Jossey-Bass.

Reed College. (2019). *Ethos of Reed*. Retrieved from https://www.reed.edu/student_life.html

Rudolph, Fred. (1965). Hopkins, Mark (1802–1887), Williams College president 1836–1872. *Williams College Alumni Review*. Retrieved from https://specialcollections.williams.edu/williams-history/presidents/hopkins-mark/

Schmidt, B. M. (2018, November 26). *The history BA since the great recession*. Retrieved from https://www.historians.org/publications-and-directories/perspectives-on-history/december-2018/the-history-ba-since-the-great-recession-the-2018-aha-majors

Schnell, Wynter. (2019). Mind, brain and behavior initiative launched at Colgate. *Colgate Maroon-News.* Retrieved from http://www.thecolgatemaroonnews.com/multimedia/article_459ae348-2a7f-11e9-ae65-2303985a9471.html

St. John's College. (2019). *Undergraduate program.* Retrieved from https://www.sjc.edu/academic-programs/undergraduate

Southern New Hampshire University. (n.d.a). *College for America.* Retrieved from https://collegeforamerica.org/

Southern New Hampshire University. (n.d.b). *History of Southern New Hampshire University.* Retrieved from https://www.snhu.edu/about-us/leadership-and-history/history

Southern New Hampshire University. (n.d.c). *About SNHU.* Retrieved from https://www.snhu.edu/about-us

Southern New Hampshire University. (n.d.d). *Three-year bachelor degrees.* Retrieved from https://www.snhu.edu/student-experience/campus-experience/campus-academics/three-year-bachelor-degrees

Southern New Hampshire University. (n.d.e). *SNHU Advantage program at Salem.* Retrieved from https://www.snhu.edu/about-us/maps-and-directions/advantage-program

Trinity Washington University. (n.d.a). *Enrollment services: Tuition and fees.* Retrieved from https://www.trinitydc.edu/enrollment/tuition-and-fees/

Trinity Washington University. (n.d.b). *Trinity's academic program.* Retrieved from https://www.trinitydc.edu/programs.

Trinity Washington University. (n.d.c). *Mission and history.* Retrieved from https://www.trinitydc.edu/mission

Trinity Washington University. (n.d.d). Envision Trinity 2020. Retrieved from https://www.trinitydc.edu/strategic-plan

U.S. Department of Education, NCES, IPEDS. (2017a). *College navigator: Agnes Scott College.* Retrieved from https://nces.ed.gov/collegenavigator/?q=Agnes+Scott&s=all&id=138600#enrolmt

U.S. Department of Education, NCES, IPEDS. (2017b). *College navigator: Dominican University of California.* Retrieved from https://nces.ed.gov/collegenavigator/?q=dominican university of californai&s=all&id=113698&fv=113698

U.S. Department of Education, NCES, IPEDS. (2017c). *College navigator: Furman University.* Retrieved from https://nces.ed.gov/collegenavigator/?q=Furman&s=all&id=218070

U.S. Department of Education, NCES, IPEDS. (2017d). *College navigator: Southern New Hampshire University.* Retrieved from https://nces.ed.gov/collegenavigator/?q=Southern+New+Hampshire+University&s=all&id=183026#retgrad

U.S. Department of Education, NCES, IPEDS. (2017e). *College navigator: Utica College.* Retrieved from https://nces.ed.gov/collegenavigator/?q=utica&s=all&id=197045

U.S. Department of Education, NCES, IPEDS. (2019a). *College navigator: California Lutheran University.* Retrieved from https://nces.ed.gov/collegenavigator/?q=california+lutheran+university&s=all&id=110413#programs

U.S. Department of Education, NCES, IPEDS. (2019b). *College navigator: Colgate University*. Retrieved from https://nces.ed.gov/collegenavigator/?q=Colgate&s=all&id=190099#programs

U.S. Department of Education, NCES, IPEDS. (2019c). *College navigator: Trinity Washington University*. Retrieved from https://nces.ed.gov/collegenavigator/?q=trinity&s=all&pg=2&id=131876#programs

Utica College. (n.d.a). *A brief history*. Retrieved from https://www.utica.edu/aboututica/brief-history

Utica College. (n.d.b). *Mission statement*. Retrieved from https://www.utica.edu/about/our-mission

Varlotta, L. (2018, Fall). Designing a model for the new liberal arts. *Liberal Education, 104*(4).

Wagner College. (2019). *The Center for Leadership & Community Engagement: Port Richmond partnership*. Retrieved from https://wagner.edu/engage/prp/

Western Interstate Commission for Higher Education. (2017). *Knocking at the college door: Profile for the nation*. Retrieved from https://knocking.wiche.edu/nation-region-profile/

Whitman College. (n.d.a). *Departments and programs*. Retrieved from https://www.whitman.edu/academics/departments-and-programs

Whitman College. (n.d.b). *Distribution requirements*. Retrieved from https://www.whitman.edu/academics/departments-and-programs/general-studies/distribution-requirements

Whitman College. (n.d.c). *Encounters*. Retrieved from https://www.whitman.edu/academics/departments-and-programs/general-studies/encounters

Whitman College. (n.d.d). *General studies*. Retrieved from https://www.whitman.edu/academics/departments-and-programs/general-studies

Whitman College. (n.d.e). *History of the college*. Retrieved from https://www.whitman.edu/about/whitman-hallmarks/history-of-the-college

Whitman College. (n.d.f). *Mission, constitution, and bylaws*. Retrieved from https://www.whitman.edu/about/mission-constitution-and-bylaws

Whitman College. (n.d.g). *Mission statement*. Retrieved from https://www.whitman.edu/about/mission-statement

Whitman College. (2017). *Whitman College strategic priorities 2017–2022*. Walla Walla, WA: Whitman College.

Whitman College. (2018). *Whitman College factbook academic year 2018–19*. Retrieved from https://www.whitman.edu/Documents/Factbook%202018%202019-02-12.pdf

Whitman College. (2019) *At a glance*. Retrieved from https://www.whitman.edu/Documents/Offices/Registrar/Catalog/Whitman%20College%20at%20a%20Glance.pdf

Wong, Frank F. (1990). *The ugly duckling of higher education*. Paper presented at the University of the Pacific, Stockton, CA.

Wylie, Margaret. (2019). *Independent colleges and projected change in high school graduates, 2017 to 2023*. Data from WICHE and The Council of Independent Colleges.

Mary B. Marcy, DPhil
President, Dominican University of California

Throughout her 27-year career in higher education leadership, Mary B. Marcy has developed major education reform and diversification initiatives, supported the advancement of faculty and students, introduced innovative programming, and enhanced the reputation and reach of the institutions she has served.

Marcy began her tenure in 2011 as the ninth president of Dominican University of California. Guided by her leadership, Dominican has gained national attention for a transformation that is rooted in creative programs, innovative partnerships, and a commitment to supporting students through a comprehensive framework for student learning and success.

As an early initiative of her presidency, Marcy began developing The Dominican Experience, a research-based and market-driven engaged learning framework for the success of every Dominican student. Throughout their undergraduate careers, students work with an integrative coach and a network of mentors; engage with the community through service-learning, internships, fieldwork, and community based research; complete a signature work; and draft a digital portfolio that assists in the transition to career or graduate school.

The Dominican Experience has led to dramatic increases in both graduation and retention rates at a time when the percentage of Dominican students identifying as ethnically diverse has increased by nearly 30 percent.

Another key area of focus has been advancing partnerships that will develop new opportunities and programs while maintaining fidelity to mission and strategic vision. Dominican is leading a first-of-its kind incubation partnership with San Francisco-based computer science academy Make

School. This is a new national model for collaboration between nonprofit higher education and the private sector to position students for success in the 21st century.

Recently, Marcy was invited by the State of California's Chief Service Officer to lead an effort to develop an innovative statewide program designed to help students pay for college through public service. The pilot California AmeriCorps Service Fellowship is due to launch in fall 2020 with a coalition of public and independent universities led by Dominican.

Marcy has presented and published extensively on the ways in which small private colleges are adapting to the rapidly changing higher education landscape. She is regularly quoted in the media related to her research and initiatives, including *The Wall Street Journal, The Washington Post, Times Higher Education, The San Francisco Chronicle, NPR, The Chronicle of Higher Education,* and *Inside Higher Education.*

In 2018, Marcy was invited to serve as a Visiting Scholar at Harvard University's Graduate School of Education. At Harvard, Marcy shared Dominican's transformation with both faculty and students, expanded her research on the future of small colleges, and further developed a book manuscript based on her 2017 *Change: The Magazine of Higher Learning* article. President Marcy's book, *The Small College Imperative,* will be released by Stylus Publishing in early 2020.

Marcy was an Arthur Vining Davis Fellow at the Aspen Ideas Festival. She has served on the Council of Independent Colleges Board of Directors and Executive Committee, and on the Steering Committee of CIC's Project on the Future of Independent Higher Education. She also is a member of the Board of Governors of the Commonwealth Club of California, the Presidents' Trust of the Association of American Colleges and Universities, and the Executive Committee of the Association of Independent California Colleges and Universities.

Prior to joining Dominican, Marcy served as Provost of Bard College at Simon's Rock and Vice President at Bard College from 2004 until 2011. Previous to her leadership at Bard, she worked in both public and private institutions of higher education. Her experience includes leading a national grant-funded Project on the Future of Higher Education through Antioch University, and serving as the lead researcher and policy advisor to the President of Western Washington University. Marcy was appointed by Massachusetts Governor Deval Patrick to serve as a commissioner on the Commonwealth's Public Education Nominating Council.

Born and raised in western Nebraska, Marcy received her Bachelor of Arts with honors from the University of Nebraska. She earned her doctorate and master's degrees in politics from the University of Oxford in the United Kingdom.